How To Work With People

Understanding Team Dynamics

Written by
Rockhurst University Continuing Education Center, Inc.
Edited by National Press Publications

NATIONAL PRESS PUBLICATIONS

A Division of Rockhurst University Continuing Education Center, Inc.
6901 West 63rd Street • P.O. Box 2949 • Shawnee Mission, Kansas 66201-1349
1-800-258-7248 • 1-913-432-7757

How to Work With People —
Understanding Team Dynamics

Published by National Press Publications, Inc.
Copyright 2000, National Press Publications, Inc.
A Division of Rockhurst University Continuing Education Center, Inc.

Printed in the United States of America

14 15 16 17 18 19 20

ISBN 1-55852-254-9

Table of Contents

INTRODUCTION

How satisfying is your job? Do you have days when you feel your career needs a complete overhaul? How well do you get along with your co-workers and those you come in contact with on a daily basis? Are there some people who just seem to rub you the wrong way?

To honestly answer these questions requires a long, hard look at yourself. Your personality traits — the way you relate to people, your likes, dislikes, skills and abilities — make you who you are. By identifying and learning about your personality, you allow your own unique traits to work for you, not against you. This understanding also becomes the key to better relationships and better communication with those around you.

The SELF Profile provides this probing insight into your personality. It consists of 30 questions that ask how you might react in given situations. Specifically the profile determines if you have a high or low need to be around people and if you have a high or low need to direct people. Based on your answers, you fall into one of four personality categories. Although you may exhibit tendencies found in all four types, you usually are dominant in one.

Simply knowing which type you are can have an immediate and positive impact on your life. If you've been contemplating a career change, the SELF Profile can help you choose a job that best suits your personality. If you've had trouble relating to someone at work, the SELF Profile can help you understand that particular co-worker's style. Conflicts can be minimized, and communication lines can be kept open.

Because people are such complex creatures, categorizing them is not the solution to every problem. However, the SELF Profile will raise your own level of self-awareness as well as your awareness of everyone around you. Ultimately, this understanding can make your life a whole lot easier and more enjoyable.

1 HOW THE SELF PROFILE CAN HELP YOU LEARN ABOUT YOURSELF AND OTHERS

You are unique. You possess an array of personality traits, skills and abilities that make you who you are. Your personality — the way you relate to others, your likes and dislikes — is the result of many years of development. Perhaps you are a perfectionist. Your house is always neat and orderly. Or maybe you are outgoing. No one remains a stranger to you for very long. When you go to a party, you spend the entire evening meeting and talking with people you don't know.

Your personality traits can work for or against you, both on the job and in your personal relationships. For example, being a perfectionist can be both positive and negative. Taking time to make sure your projects are perfect is positive. However, if you take so much time making sure your projects are perfect that you are consistently late turning them in, your perfectionism becomes a negative factor.

Being good at solving conflicts is positive if it means that you are able to negotiate a reasonable solution with your customer. If, however, you solve the conflict regardless of the cost to the company, it can be negative.

No one personality style is better than another. But different personality types often have a difficult time relating to each other. The key is to learn as much as you can about your personality traits and those of the people you deal with regularly. If you do, you will be better able to communicate with others, and often you can avoid conflict before it arises.

Your Personality Traits and Other People

How you relate to other people depends largely on your personality. For example, if you enjoy spontaneity and surprises, you may be excited about the prospect of "kidnapping" your spouse and taking him away on a romantic weekend. If, however, your spouse is more level-headed and practical, he is not going to respond very enthusiastically to being whisked away. He will be uncomfortable because his personality has a need to plan. As a result, what was supposed to be a fun-filled weekend will turn into a stressful time for both of you. Does this mean that you and your husband aren't meant for each other?

By the same token, perhaps you enjoy helping others and can't say no when a co-worker asks for a hand. Generally, this is seen as positive. But what if your boss doesn't appreciate your helping others when you have work of your own to do? Does this mean that you can't help others?

The answer to both of the above questions is no. The trick is to learn to use your personality traits so that they work *for* you, not *against* you.

Learning More About Your Personality Traits

Learning more about yourself and others will help you relieve some of the stress that you encounter in your daily life. The more you understand why you react the way you do in given situations and why others react the way they do, the more you will understand how to cope with these situations when they arise. Coping positively gives you control over those personality factors that have caused you stress in the past.

The only person you can control is yourself. You can't change your boss who is insensitive, your co-worker who is satisfied doing mediocre work or your spouse who is critical. But if you understand the certain personality traits of others that make them the way they are, it will be easier for you to interact with these people in your life.

This handbook is designed to help you learn about your personality traits and those of others. By taking the SELF Profile included in Chapter 2, you will discover your personal characteristics. This information will help you understand why you react the way you do in certain situations.

You will also be able to take this information and apply it to others. By doing this, you will be better able to appreciate the differences between yourself and others instead of using these differences as a point of contention. This appreciation results in better relationships, less stress and harmony instead of conflict.

What Is the SELF Profile?

The SELF Profile is a questionnaire that helps you learn about your personal characteristics. It consists of 30 questions describing how an individual might act in given situations. Based on an individual's answers, the respondent is then placed in one of four quadrants which indicate personality styles. By carefully studying this information, you can use it to recognize both your and others' personality styles to interact more effectively in relationships.

Different Personality Styles

If you've ever experienced the death of a loved one, you know that everyone reacts differently. One person may openly cry and grieve at the funeral while another sits quietly, almost passively, in the corner. One person surrounds himself with friends and family, while the other prefers to be alone. Neither is grieving more. Each is handling the situation in the best way he knows how.

The same is true with most situations in our lives. Everyone reacts differently. Let's look at the following example. The boss tells Bob and Mary to work together with the other members of their department to develop a proposal for a client. Bob, who prefers to work alone, immediately goes to his office and starts making copious notes. Mary, on the other hand, calls her co-workers together and suggests they go out for drinks after work to "throw some ideas around." When she mentions it to Bob, he gets angry and mumbles something about doing it by himself.

Bob, because of his more analytical, reserved nature feels that Mary is wasting time and that they will never get the job done. Mary, on the other hand, feels that Bob is trying to "go off on his own tangent" and not let anyone else in the department have a say.

If Bob and Mary were aware of their personality traits ahead of time, they probably could work out an agreeable situation. For example, since Mary is more outgoing, she might agree to get the department together to generate ideas on what they might do. And, since Bob is more information-oriented, he might be in charge of taking the information from the group and putting it together in a workable proposal.

What You Will Learn From This Handbook

In order to learn how to make your personality traits work for you, you must first identify your distinct personality style. You can do this by taking the SELF Profile.

The SELF Profile is designed to help you better understand yourself and others. It will also help you learn how to be more flexible so that you can deal effectively with others. Armed with the information you gain through the SELF Profile, you will have a better idea of why you react the way you do. And once you apply what you have learned to others, you will have some insight as to why they behave the way they do.

The goal of this book is to help you develop your strengths and create greater awareness between all four styles of the SELF Profile.

After you take the SELF Profile and apply the information you will:

- Create an environment where you feel comfortable.

- Lower your stress level and thus get more work accomplished.

- Build an atmosphere of confidence and trust with others.

- Make yourself and others feel psychologically safe.

- Work more effectively with others.

2 TAKING THE SELF PROFILE

By taking the SELF Profile, you will learn your personality style and how to make it work for you.

The SELF Profile will help you:

- Identify your particular style.

- Gain a better understanding of yourself and others.

- Predict how you and others might respond in given situations.

- Improve your communications with others who have different styles from yours.

In taking the SELF Profile, it is important to remember that it is simply a guideline. Most people, depending on what is happening in their lives at the time, will flex between a couple of the four styles. You may even find that you possess the qualities of several of the styles. However, more than likely, you will find that you are more dominant in one of the four styles.

The SELF Profile consists of 30 general questions describing how you might respond in a given situation. It takes approximately 10 minutes to complete. In answering these questions, don't spend too much time contemplating your answers; your first reaction is generally your best.

In answering questions one through 24, use the following scale. If you think the statement is not at all like you, mark number 1. If you think it is very much like you, mark 5.

1	2	3	4	5
Not at all like me	Somewhat like me	Occasionally like me	Usually like me	Very Much like me

_____ 1. When in a group, I tend to speak and act as the representative of that group.

_____ 2. I am seldom quiet when I am with other people.

_____ 3. When faced with a leadership position, I tend to actively accept that role rather than diffuse it among others.

_____ 4. I would rather meet new people than read a good book.

_____ 5. Sometimes I ask more from my friends or family than they can accomplish.

_____ 6. I enjoy going out frequently.

_____ 7. It's important to me that people follow the advice that I give them.

_____ 8. I like to entertain guests.

_____ 9. When I am in charge of a situation, I am comfortable assigning others to specific tasks.

_____ 10. I often go out of my way to meet new people.

_____ 11. In social settings, I find myself asking more questions of others than they ask of me.

_____ 12. I truly enjoy mixing in a crowd.

_____ 13. Other people usually think of me as being energetic.

_____ 14. I make friends very easily.

_____ 15. I am a verbal person.

_____ 16. I try to be supportive of my friends, no matter what they do.

_____ 17. If I see it's not going smoothly in a group, I usually take the lead and try to bring some structure to the situation.

_____ 18. I seldom find it hard to really enjoy myself at a lively party.

_____ 19. When in a leadership position, I like to clearly define my role and let followers know what is expected.

_____ 20. I consider myself to be good at small talk.

_____ 21. I am very good at persuading others to see things my way.

_____ 22. I can usually let myself go and have fun with friends.

_____ 23. I often find myself playing the role of leader and taking charge of the situation.

_____ 24. I do not prefer the simple, quiet life.

For questions 25-30, circle the letter representing your response.

25. You are in a conversation with more than one person. Someone makes a statement that you know is incorrect, but you are sure the others didn't catch it. Do you let the others know?

   A. Yes

   B. No

26. After a hard day's work I prefer to:

   A. Get together with a few friends and do something active.

   B. Relax at home and either watch TV or read.

27. When planning a social outing with a small group, I am most likely to:

    A. Be the first to suggest some plans and try to get the others to make a decision quickly.

    B. Make sure everyone has a say in the planning and go along with what the group decides.

28. You have just finished a three-month project for which you have sacrificed a great deal of your free time and energy. To celebrate, are you more likely to:

    A. Invite some of your friends over and throw a party.

    B. Spend a quiet, peaceful weekend doing whatever you wish, either by yourself or with a special friend.

29. If I feel that I am underpaid for my work, I'm most likely to:

    A. Confront the boss and demand a raise.

    B. Do nothing and hope the situation improves.

30. I think those around me see me as primarily:

    A. Gregarious and outgoing.

    B. Introspective and thoughtful.

Scoring the SELF Profile

Transfer your scores from questions 1–24 onto the grid below. For questions 25–30 give yourself a 5 for every A and a 1 for every B. Now add each column and record the total for each column as the directive and affiliative totals.

1. _____	2. _____
3. _____	4. _____
5. _____	6. _____
7. _____	8. _____
9. _____	10. _____
11. _____	12. _____
13. _____	14. _____
15. _____	16. _____
17. _____	18. _____
19. _____	20. _____
21. _____	22. _____
23. _____	24. _____
25. _____	26. _____
27. _____	28. _____
29. _____	30. _____

Directive Total _____   **Affiliative Total** _____

Using the scoring chart below, convert your Directive and Affiliative totals from the previous page. Then record your converted directive and affiliative score (one through six) in the space provided just below the scoring chart.

If you scored from:	Give yourself a:
15-21	1
22-33	2
34-44	3
45-56	4
57-68	5
69-75	6

Converted Directive Score _____   **Converted Affiliative Score** _____

- On the graph at the top of the next page put a dot on the vertical (broken) line next to the number that is the same as your Converted Directive Score.

- Put a dot on the horizontal (dotted) line next to the number that is the same as your Converted Affiliative Score.

- Connect the two dots with a straight line.

- Now shade in the area of the triangle you've created.

Your SELF Profile Graph

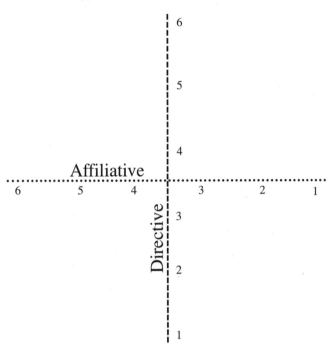

What It All Means

Now that you've scored your profile, what does it all mean? The dotted, horizontal line represents your Affiliative Score. It measures your needs and desires for being around other people. If you scored high on this line (a four or above), you enjoy working with other people. If you scored low on this scale (a three or below), you probably are not as outgoing and, when given the opportunity, prefer to work independently.

The broken, vertical line represents your Directive Score. It measures your needs and tendencies to direct and control situations. If you scored high on this scale (a four or above), it indicates that you tend to be comfortable meeting others and controlling situations. If you scored low on the Directive Scale (a three or below), it means that you are less comfortable directing: you tend to be supportive and prefer to seek consensus from others before proceeding.

The higher or lower you are on these scales, the more likely you are to have the tendencies indicated. For example, if you scored a six on the Affiliative Scale, you probably have a high need to work with others. This information can be helpful to you in choosing a job. The higher you scored on the Affiliative Scale, the more likely you would be satisfied in a job which included contact with others. On the other hand, if you scored a one on the Affiliative Scale, you would prefer a job where you had little or no contact with others. With a low Affiliative Score, you prefer to work alone and probably would not enjoy a job as a public relations representative or a retail salesperson — just the jobs that would appeal to the high Affiliative scorer.

If you scored near the middle of either scale (a three or a four), you will tend to be more flexible and will find that you have the characteristics of more than one quadrant. For example, if you score a four on the Directive Scale, you probably don't mind running a meeting or being in charge of the church social, but you don't feel compelled to do it. You would probably be just as happy chairing a task force that's an offshoot of the committee or operating a booth at the social. Or if you scored a three on the Affiliative Score, you probably prefer to work alone, but would still feel comfortable working in a small group.

It is important to note, however, that your scores represent *preference*, not ability or skill. This test does not identify abilities!

Four Preference Quadrants

To help readily identify the four quadrants, we are going to give them names. If your triangle falls in the upper left-hand quadrant, you are an S. If your triangle falls in the upper right-hand quadrant, you are an E. If your triangle falls in the lower left-hand quadrant, you are an L. If your triangle falls in the lower right-hand quadrant, you are an F.

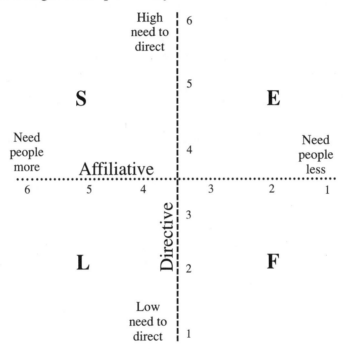

Changing Styles

S-E-L-F, self. To be a fully functioning and effective communicator you must, and do, access all four aspects of your personality. For some people, one aspect dominates and creates a very definitive style. For others, their preferences are less defined and their styles may blend.

Just because you scored high in one quadrant today doesn't mean you would get the same score if you took the profile in six months. You can flip-flop from one style to another depending on what is happening in your life at the time. These are just tendencies. They are not cast in stone, but generally you will favor one style, preferring it over the other three.

Conclusion

Now that you know which quadrant indicates your style, you will learn more about the characteristics, strengths, weaknesses, likes and dislikes and working strategies of that style. Remember, no one style is better than another.

In a survey of companies, it was found that CEOs were equally divided among the quadrants. The difference seemed to be in the type of company each CEO ran.

- Ss tend to head organizations that promote, sell and entertain.

- Es tend to head sales organizations such as telemarketing companies, retail stores, etc.

- Ls tend to head service-oriented organizations that help people such as health care, insurance, etc.

- Fs tend to head analytical organizations such as computer companies, engineering companies, etc.

3 STRENGTHS OF THE FOUR STYLES

Go back to your graph in Chapter 2 and examine it carefully. Are you an S, E, L or F? Now look at the area that you shaded in. Is it relatively large, as in Figure 1 below, or is it small, as in Figures 2 and 3?

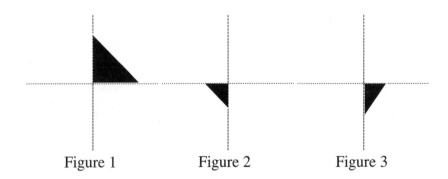

Figure 1　　　　Figure 2　　　　Figure 3

Generally, the larger the shaded area, the more likely you are to possess the tendencies of that style. The smaller the area, the more likely you are to be flexible in given situations and the better able you will be to adapt to a social style. For example, if you scored a three or four on the Directive Scale, you can lead the meeting, if asked. But you are probably just as able to adapt to being a participant.

Depending on which quadrant you fall in, you will have certain characteristics that describe your tendencies, such as risk-taker, traditional, trusting or meticulous. Learning your particular strengths and weaknesses will help you adapt your style to work more effectively with others and develop more positive personal relationships. Learning about the strengths and weaknesses of others enhances your personal and working relationships with them.

Common Characteristics of the Four Dimensions

As you will notice in the chart below, when the broken and dotted lines intersect, they form four dimensions. As noted in Chapter 2, these dimensions are known as S, E, L and F.

STRENGTHS

	High	
S		**E**
Persuasive		Practical
Risk-taker		Orderly
Competitive		Very direct
Pursues change		Self-determined
Confident		Organized
Socially skilled		Traditional
Inspiring		Goal-oriented
Open		Dependable
Direct		Economical
Outgoing		Ambitious

AFFILIATIVE

High		**Low**
L	DIRECTIVE	**F**
Team-oriented		Exacting
Caring		Thorough
Devoted		Factual
Enthusiastic		Reserved
Helpful		Meticulous
Accessible		Practical
Trusting		Calm
Sensitive		Has high standards
Good listener		Risk-avoider
Good friend		
Likes variety	**Low**	
Gregarious		
Peacemaker		

In this chapter, we will examine the strengths of each of the four dimensions.

Strengths of the S Preference

If you are in the "S" quadrant, you scored high on the Affiliative Scale and high on the Directive Scale. You are a natural leader; people want to follow you. You are not, however, a detail person. Whenever possible, you delegate that job to someone else.

Ss tend to be social. In the workplace you are most likely to find an S at the coffee pot talking with co-workers about the best way to solve the latest disaster or how to go about completing a project. At a party, they are the individuals who attract attention.

Here are some characteristics that typically describe the tendencies of the S Preference:

- *Persuasive* — You can talk anybody into anything. For example, you want to go out dancing, but your spouse says he is too tired. He worked 20 hours overtime this week. You can convince him by telling him going out is just what he needs to relax and you won't stay out too late.

- *Risk-taker* — You are not only willing to take risks, you enjoy taking them. Your boss asks for a volunteer to be project leader for Tip Top Freezer Company. You know that the president of Tip Top has fired his last two advertising firms in less than a year. Your boss stresses that it will be the responsibility of whoever takes on the project to keep the client happy. You gladly accept the challenge and probably several others along the way.

- *Competitive* — Competition spurs you on. You work best in an environment where your successes and failures, and those of your co-workers, are measured. You are the first one to sign up for the company softball team, accept a dare or take on a challenge.

- *Pursues Change* — You don't enjoy doing the same thing. You like a job where you do different tasks every day. In your personal relationships, you tend to have lots of friends, instead of just a handful of close ones.

- *Confident* — Can you do the job? Of course you can. Just ask you. Your motto in life is, "Never say never." If the boss asks, "Can you do …" your immediate response is always, "Yes."

- *Socially Skilled* — It's not a problem to you if your boss asks you to attend a cocktail party where you will know no one. You welcome the opportunity and soon find yourself in the middle of the group. You enjoy the limelight and actually search it out.

- *Inspiring* — Your friends come to you when they need a boost. You know just the right thing to say to get them motivated and stirred up.

- *Open and Direct* — You don't beat around the bush. If a co-worker asks you what you think of a report he just spent weeks working on, you will tell him in no uncertain terms. If you feel that it is good, you will tell him why. But if you think it is poor, you will show no mercy.

- *Outgoing* — People seem to be naturally drawn to you and you, likewise, gladly approach new people.

Strengths of the E Quadrant

If you are an E, you scored low on the Affiliative Scale, but high on the Directive Scale. You have good ideas, but tend to be practical. You have lots of ambition and you are dependable. When it comes to getting things done, you have tunnel vision and will move heaven and earth to finish the job. You are bottom-line oriented. With a low score on the Affiliative Scale, you are not a real people-person. You don't let people get in your way if you have to get the job done.

Es are so goal-oriented that they sometimes tune out whatever doesn't affect the bottom line. For example, if an E boss calls you in and asks you for the latest sales figures, he only wants the figures. If you also tell him about a big sale you just made, don't be surprised if two hours later when you ask him about your new client, he acts like he has no idea what you're talking about. Es listen for what they need in order to get the job done and tune out the rest.

If you are an E, you will probably recognize yourself in these adjectives:

- *Practical* — In your personal life, you are not much of a romantic. For your wedding anniversary you can't understand why your wife wants to go back to the restaurant where you first met when you have a coupon for a perfectly fine restaurant in town.

- *Orderly* — When people walk into your office, they might question whether you even work there. The top of your desk is clear, and papers are filed neatly in your file cabinets.

- *Very Direct* — You are direct, sometimes to the point of being abrasive. If your girlfriend is wearing a new dress that you don't like, you might take one look at her and say, "You're not wearing that to the party, are you?"

- *Self-determined* — You know what you want, and you go after it. You don't need plaques or special perks to help you succeed: your satisfaction comes from doing a good job and knowing it. Unlike the S, who likes to receive plaques, trophies and other indications of a job well done, the E's true reward is knowing he has reached his quota.

- *Organized* — You are the organizer. When you go on vacation you have every detail of your trip planned ahead of time. You know exactly where you are going to be when, and before you even leave the house, you know exactly how much money you will spend.

- *Traditional* — Your idea of a perfect Christmas is gathering the family together for a huge meal — just like your family did when you were growing up. You would never dream of taking a cruise or going on a ski vacation over the Christmas holidays, unless that's what you always did when you were growing up.

- *Goal-oriented* — You enjoy setting goals and then establishing action plans to achieve them. You work best in a job setting which includes quotas and goals. You want to get the job done, and you want it done now.

- *Dependable* — If you say you will do it, it will be done. Your boss knows that if you tell him the job will be done by the end of the workday, it will be done by the end of the workday. He never has to check up on you.

- *Economical* — At the grocery store, you carry your coupons in a pouch with dividers. Before you pick up any product, you look to see if you have a coupon. When a friend calls and asks you to go to lunch, you respond, "Wait just a minute and let me see if I have any coupons."

- *Ambitious* — You're not content to stay at a job if you feel it is going nowhere. Whenever you feel like you have gone as far as you can in your job, you begin to look for other opportunities within your company or outside. Once you reach a goal, you set a new one and immediately set out to achieve it.

Strengths of the L Preference

If you are an L, you scored high on the Affiliative Scale and low on the Directive Scale. You are a team player. You are a caring person, and, contrary to the E, you are an excellent listener. You listen to what is not being said as well as to what is being said. The minute your spouse walks into the house, you can tell what kind of a day he has had.

Your friends and co-workers see you as the caretaker. You are the person in the office whom everyone comes to with their problems. You want everyone to be happy, so much so that you sometimes become passive and allow others to take advantage of you.

If you are in the L quadrant, here are some of the strengths you probably possess:

- *Team-oriented* — You prefer to play team sports, like volleyball and softball, rather than individual sports, such as golf or tennis. On the job, you enjoy situations where you can work with others in order to complete a project. You enjoy serving on task forces and committees.

- *Caring* — You take the feelings of others into consideration before you act. If an employee comes to you and says he has to leave because his child is sick, your first concern is for the employee and his child. You don't worry about the fact that he is in the middle of a project which has to be done by the end of the day. Instead, you will probably complete the project yourself.

- *Devoted* — Whether it's on the job or in a relationship, you are totally devoted. In a relationship, your partner or spouse never has to worry about your straying. At work, your boss knows that you will never leave him in a bind.

- *Enthusiastic* — Everybody wants you on their team. You have a certain spark that can get everyone else going. You enthusiastically embrace every project that you tackle, as if it is the most important project you've ever done.

- *Helpful* — When someone in the office says they need a hand, you are the first one to offer assistance. Even if you are in the midst of a crisis yourself, you will drop what you are doing to help out someone else.

- *Accessible* — Your friends and co-workers know that you will always be there for them. If you are the boss, you have an open-door policy. Your employees always feel encouraged to come and talk to you.

- *Trusting* — Your friends feel comfortable telling you their innermost secrets. They know that if they ask you not to tell anyone, you won't. Your boss often shares privileged information with you.

- *Sensitive* — As an L, you tend to take things personally. For example, if someone questions the way you approached a project, you immediately become defensive and assume they are saying you didn't do it right.

- *Good Listener* — In conversations with others, you sometimes appear quiet. Actually, you are listening intently to what they are saying.

- *Good Friend* — You are the type of individual whom anyone would like to have as a friend. You are always there — during good times and bad.

- *Likes Variety* — You prefer a job with a multitude of responsibilities. It doesn't bother you to juggle several things at once. You would be bored if you had to do the same thing every day.

- *Gregarious* — Your laugh is infectious. In fact, your co-workers may even tease you because they can hear you laughing down the hall. Actually, that is one of the things they like about you. You enjoy life, and you're not afraid to show it.

- *Peacemaker* — You don't like dissension — in the office or in your personal life. If two people in the office or two friends are having a disagreement, you are the one who will most likely step in and try to help them find common ground.

Strengths of the F Preference

If you are an F, you scored low on the Affiliative Scale and low on the Directive Scale. You are analytical. You would be perfectly content working in a research lab where there are no other people around. As far as you are concerned, it doesn't matter how long something takes to get done, as long as it is done right. You have very high standards for yourself and others.

You don't like taking risks. You are most comfortable with the status quo. Your biggest fear is being wrong. If things don't go your way, you tend to withdraw.

If you are an F, here are some adjectives which describe you:

- *Exacting* — To you "close enough" just isn't good enough. Whenever you do something, it has to be 100 percent right. You were the kind of child in school who wouldn't turn in an assignment with a cross-out on it. If you made a mistake, you started over, no matter how long it took you to get it right.

- *Thorough* — When you do a job, you do it well. If your boss asks you to take inventory, you will count everything twice — just to make sure you didn't miss anything.

- *Factual* — If your boss asks you to research something, he doesn't have to worry about whether or not it will be accurate. He knows that you won't give him any information unless it is backed by the facts.

- *Reserved* — At parties, you tend to stand back and wait until someone talks to you. It isn't in your nature to approach people you don't know and start a conversation.

- *Meticulous* — Your desk, your home, even your drawers are neat and orderly. Your towels in your linen closet are folded perfectly. You can't stand to have things out of place.

- *Practical* — Like the E, you are practical. For example, you probably can't understand why anyone would go to the stadium to watch a football game when they can watch it in the comfort of their own home.

- *Calm* — It takes a lot to ruffle your feathers. In a crisis, you are the one who steps in and takes charge.

- *Has High Standards* — You expect a lot out of yourself and others. Like the E, you have a strong desire to get the job done. However, when you do a job, it has to be done right.

- *Risk-avoider* — You don't like taking risks. When a new way of doing things is introduced at work, you prefer to do it the old way until the new way has been tried and proven.

Conclusion

Each style has its own particular strengths. By knowing these strengths both for yourself and for others, you can use them to your advantage. For example, ask the E to arrange the staff luncheon; give the master-of-ceremonies job to the S, and let the L get everyone involved. Your F staff member will have to be convinced to attend, but once there, he will easily handle the money details!

By being aware of the strengths of each style, you can benefit from them and ensure that people feel comfortable and secure with you.

4 WEAKNESSES OF THE FOUR STYLES

As each dimension has strengths that are associated with it, each also has some limitations or weaknesses. Often, our weaknesses are simply strengths carried to extremes. For example, being goal-oriented is a positive attribute. If, however, you don't care whether or not you hurt others while attaining your goals, it becomes a negative attribute.

LIMITATIONS

	High	
S		**E**
Pushy		Dogmatic
Intimidating		Stubborn
Overbearing		Rigid
Restless		Unapproachable
Impatient		Distant
Manipulative		Critical
Abrasive		Insensitive
Reactive		
Dominating		

AFFILIATIVE

High		**Low**
L		**F**
Too other-oriented		Slow to get things done
Indecisive		Perfectionistic
Impractical		Withdrawn
Vulnerable		Dull
Hesitant		Sullen
Subjective		Shy
		Passive

DIRECTIVE

Low

In this chapter, you will learn about your weaknesses. Knowing your weaknesses will help you learn to be more flexible with others and more tolerant of their weaknesses too. Since weaknesses often lead to conflict, knowing them before you enter into an interaction with another person assists you in avoiding interpersonal conflicts.

Knowing the weaknesses of others will help you understand why they react the way they do. For example, if you are working with someone who is indecisive, knowing that indecision is a characteristic weakness of her personality type will help you work with her to overcome it. Following are the weaknesses characteristic of each of the four styles.

Limitations of the S Personality

Even though you are socially skilled, some of your strengths can work against you, and you may find yourself being viewed as pushy, manipulative or abrasive.

If you are an S, here are some of your limitations:

- *Pushy* — Because you are so self-assured and competitive, some people may see you as pushy. For example, if every time your boss asks for someone to take charge of a project you immediately step in, another employee who really wants to take on the task, but isn't quite as confident, may perceive you as pushy.

- *Intimidating* — Your self-assurance can also make you appear quite intimidating. Someone less confident than you may actually shy away from working with you. This can also be a problem in personal relationships. For example, if you are an S woman, you may find it difficult to interact with some men who find you intimidating.

- *Overbearing* — Taken the wrong way, your directness may make some people view you as overbearing. Because you "tell it like it is," you sometimes appear to be insensitive to others.

- *Restless* — You enjoy change, but sometimes a little too much. Sometimes you don't even have one job done before you start looking for something else to do. If you find yourself paired with an F who prides herself on being thorough, you may encounter a conflict as she strives for perfection and you push for completion so that you can move on to something else.

- *Impatient* — You're the person at the checkout line in the grocery store who is scanning every piece of reading material in the racks. You hate to wait. You seldom go anywhere without things to do if you must wait. You become extremely irritated at work if meetings don't begin or end on time.

- *Manipulative* — You are persuasive but sometimes to an extreme. As a result, you become manipulative. For example, you and a co-worker, John, are supposed to work on a project together. John is an F and extremely meticulous. You would have preferred working with Larry, who is an S like you. When your boss asks how things are going you say, "Oh, not bad. I feel kind of sorry for John, though. He doesn't really have a lot of spare time right now, and this new project is really bogging him down. By the way, Larry was telling me he's got so little going on in his department, he's bored."

- *Abrasive* — Because you are impatient, you sometimes seem abrasive. When a co-worker comes to a meeting 10 minutes late, you probably won't even greet her when she walks in the office but simply say, "Okay, let's get started."

- *Reactive* — You often react to situations before you've had a chance to think them through. For example, if your husband tells you he wants to buy a new car, you immediately snap and respond, "We can't afford a new car." You don't give him an opportunity to explain why he thinks a new car is needed at this time.

- *Dominating* — You are so outgoing and chatty that others sometimes feel as if they can't get a word in. As a result, they may consider you to be dominating the conversation and the group.

Limitations of the E Personality

As an E, you are ambitious and goal-oriented. These are traits that are normally viewed as positives. If, however, you take them to extremes, you may be viewed as distant, rigid and unapproachable.

If you are an E, here are some weaknesses you will want to address:

- *Dogmatic* — Regardless of the conversation, you are right. For example, your co-worker comes to you and says that she believes the boss wanted the project completed a different way. You really aren't sure, but your immediate reaction is to snap, "No, she doesn't. I'm doing it right."

- *Stubborn* — You won't even try looking at things a different way. You believe you are right, and that's the end of it.

- *Rigid* — Things have to be done *your* way. This can cause you trouble, especially at work. For example, if the boss tells you you must do something a different way at work and you insist that you are going to continue to do it your own way, you may be viewed as insubordinate and eventually lose your job.

- *Unapproachable* — Because of the weaknesses already discussed, some people may view you as unapproachable. They feel that you are closed to any further interaction on a subject.

- *Distant* — You are extremely goal-oriented. All you can see is your goal, and you won't let anything get in your way. If an employee comes in and tells you that his father just died, your response may be, "So how will that affect your completing the project you're working on?"

- *Critical* — You are critical. As far as you are concerned, no one can do things as well as you can. You criticize everyone.

- *Insensitive* — You are not a good people-person. If an employee comes into your office with a personal problem, you don't know how to handle it. The result is that, more often than not, the employee leaves thinking you just don't care.

Limitations of the L Personality

Unlike Es, the Ls love people. Their high Affiliative score means they love working with other people. Sometimes, however, their sensitivity to other people can get in the way of getting the job done.

If you are an L, here are some of your weaknesses:

- *Too other-oriented* — Ranking high on the Affiliative Scale, you are a devoted, trusting friend. However, being too other-oriented can also work against you. For example, you are the type of individual who will help anyone in the office who needs a hand. Sometimes, this becomes a problem when you can't get your own work done.

- *Indecisive* — You are so team-oriented that you always want to get everyone else's opinion before making a decision. If you take this too far, however, you become indecisive and may have a problem getting the job done.

- *Impractical* — You have such a high need to be loved that you can sometimes be frivolous. For example, you spend $200 on a gift for your husband, then don't have the money to pay the electric bill.

- *Vulnerable* — You are so trusting that others may take advantage of you. For example, if someone in your office wants a job you know all about and expect to get, she may play up to you and pretend to be your friend. You buy into it, and she snatches your job right out from underneath you.

- *Hesitant* — You don't make quick decisions. Instead, you tend to hold back and see what happens. In situations where an immediate decision is needed, you have problems.

- *Subjective* — You base your judgments on feelings instead of facts. For example, an employee comes to you and wants the next day off to attend her daughter's play at school. You know you are going to be short-handed because another employee is going to be on vacation, but you let her go because you want to be fair. As a result, you end up working overtime the next day to make up for the personnel shortage.

Limitations of the F Personality

On the "strengths" side, Fs tend to be thorough and meticulous. But when taken to extremes, this behavior can become perfectionistic, causing them to do things so slowly that they have difficulty getting things accomplished. Fs need to guard against becoming workaholics. Even though they may delegate work to others, when it is returned they check and recheck it.

If you are an F, the following are some of your weaknesses:

- *Slow to Get Things Done* — You are so precise and meticulous that you often miss deadlines. You won't turn in a report until everything has met your high standard of perfection.

- *Perfectionistic* — You take perfectionism to extremes. You become obsessive in your quest to get everything right.

- *Withdrawn* — Scoring low on the Affiliative Scale, you are not a real people-person. You prefer to work alone, and as a result, you tend to keep to yourself. Others may view this as unsociable.

- *Dull* — Because you are not outgoing, people don't get to see the real you. As a result, some people may consider you to be dull.

- *Sullen* — You can be very annoyed when people fail to meet your high standards. However, your tendency to keep to yourself means that you may say nothing, but show your displeasure by refusing to take part in the discussion. To others, this may appear as sullen behavior on your part.

- *Shy* — In a crowd, you can be found in the corner, usually alone. You have no desire to mingle with people you don't know. As a result of your shyness, you may actually miss meeting a lot of interesting people.

- *Passive* — With a low score on the Directive Scale, you are more than willing to let others go their way and do your own work your way.

Conclusion

Your weaknesses tell you as much about yourself as your strengths. By knowing your weaknesses, you can work to turn them into strengths.

To help you put to use what you learned in Chapters 3 and 4, do the following exercise:

1) List three strengths of your SELF dimension that are most like you.

   _____

   _____

   _____

2) Select two limitations that most accurately describe you.

   _____

   _____

3) Think of a situation in which you are most likely to act in a manner characteristic of your dimension. Now think of a situation where you might take on the characteristics of another dimension. List the situation and the dimension.

   _____

   _____

   _____

4) List at least one adjective from each dimension that you consider a strength you possess in that style.

S   _____

E   _____

L   _____

F   _____

5 LIKES AND DISLIKES OF THE FOUR STYLES

We all have turn-ons and turn-offs — things we like and things we don't like. When we encounter things that we like on the job, they motivate us to do a good job. When we encounter things that we don't like, we tend not to do a good job.

Turn-ons, or things that you like, make you feel psychologically safe. They are the things that make you feel good about yourself and make you want to do a good job.

Turn-offs, or things that you don't like, on the other hand, make you feel psychologically uncertain. If you experience too many turn-offs, you will not do a good job.

By knowing the turn-ons and turn-offs for the four styles, you can develop an atmosphere that is psychologically safe for you and others.

TURN-ONS

	High	
S		**E**
Attention		Control
Achievement		Responsibility
Recognition		Mastery
Adventure		Loyalty
Excitement		Fast pace
Spontaneity		

AFFILIATIVE

High — Low

L		**F**
Popularity		Perfection
Closeness		Autonomy
Affirmation	**DIRECTIVE**	Consistency
Kindness		Practical things
Caring		Information

Low

TURN-OFFS

	High	
S		**E**
Lack of enthusiasm		Ambiguity
Waiting		Irreverence
Indecision		Laziness
Convention		Showing emotions

AFFILIATIVE

High — Low

L		**F**
Insensitivity		Over-assertiveness
Dissension		Carelessness
Insincerity	**DIRECTIVE**	Arrogance
Egotism		Fakes

Low

Turn-Ons for the S

Ss need attention, achievement, recognition, adventure, excitement and spontaneity to make them feel comfortable in their work environment. They are the ones you turn to if you need a meeting planned in five minutes.

Following are some of the things that motivate or turn on the S:

- *Attention* — You love to be the center of attention. You usually speak up and express your opinion just so everyone will notice you.

- *Achievement* — You don't mind working hard if you can see what you have achieved. For example, if you are a writer, you love the thrill you get from seeing your article published or your book in print.

- *Recognition* — You have plaques and trophies all over your office. You've worked hard to earn them, and you want to show them off. Viewing your awards gives you the motivation to work even harder.

- *Adventure* — You thrive on adventure. You would much rather spend the weekend white-water rafting than in a cozy little Bed and Breakfast.

- *Excitement* — You love excitement. In fact, the more the better. Sometimes, this can be hard on your relationships as you strive to bring excitement into them.

- *Spontaneity* — You love throwing impromptu dinner parties and being asked to do spur-of-the-moment activities. You can throw things together at the last minute and still have them turn out well.

Turn-Ons for the E

Es need control. In fact, their greatest fear is losing control. That's why Es often don't make good patients in the hospital. They need to have control of themselves and others. However, they are always in such a hurry to get things done they sometimes miss important details.

If you are an E, here are some of the things that are turn-ons for you:

- *Control* — The higher your score on the Directive Scale, the more need you have for control. You are extremely self-determined. The only way you can ensure that you achieve your goals is to have total control.

- *Responsibility* — You are responsible and like to be given assignments that test your sense of responsibility. You are happiest when your boss assigns you a project and then walks away and lets you complete it without supervision.

- *Mastery* — You like to master skills. If you are a salesperson, for example, you find it challenging to learn everything you can about the product you are selling. You will also spend hours learning about your clients.

- *Loyalty* — You are traditional. You are loyal, and you expect loyalty from those with whom you work.

- *Fast Pace* — You never sit still. You may feel constrained in a job sitting behind a desk all day. You prefer jobs where you have more than enough to keep you busy.

Turn-Ons for the L

Ls want to be liked. They want closeness and feeling part of a team. Regardless of the job, they want to feel they are making a major contribution to the overall team effort.

If you are an L, here are things that you view as turn-ons:

- *Popularity* — You not only seek popularity, you need it. Knowing that others like you is important to you.

- *Closeness* — You work well in group settings. You like to have people around you. You wouldn't enjoy a job where you worked alone and had no contact with others.

- *Affirmation* — You like to be told that you are doing a good job. It makes you feel appreciated and reaffirms your confidence in yourself.

- *Kindness* — You are a sincere, caring person, and you appreciate the kindness of others. If you do a favor for a friend, you are pleased when that individual does something nice for you in return.

- *Caring* — You really like being around thoughtful people: the co-worker who puts flowers on your desk on your birthday; the people in your department who take up a collection for a needy family at Christmas; the boss who suggests you go home early because you have a sick child at the baby-sitter.

Turn-Ons for the F

Fs tend to be perfectionists. They would rather work alone than with a group of people. They also like consistency, and they like the status quo. Don't paint an F's office over the weekend or take things off the top of the desk. F's need information. If you want them to do a project, explain to them in meticulous detail what is needed.

Following are some of your likes, if you are an F:

- *Perfection* — You do things perfectly, and you expect the same of others. You would never purchase anything that was not totally perfect. When you buy clothes, you turn them inside out to make sure every seam is sewn perfectly.

- *Autonomy* — You really don't care for work groups at the office. You would much rather be given a project and then left alone to complete it. You don't want to have to rely on others.

- *Consistency* — You don't like it when the rules change. Once you know how something is to be done, you don't want the rules to change two days later.

- *Practical Things* — You like ideas only when they are practical. Theory is fine for some, but you want to know exactly how it will work in the real world.

- *Information* — As far as you are concerned, the more information, the better. You can't have too much information.

Turn-Offs for the S

Ss don't like convention. Their philosophy in life is "rules are made to be broken." You are an extremely energetic, confident person. It really bothers you if others don't show the same level of excitement.

- *Lack of Enthusiasm* — You have a great deal of enthusiasm for everything in life. It infuriates you if someone acts indifferent to something that you think is important.

- *Waiting* — You have so much energy you can't sit still. You find waiting intolerable. You are prompt, and you have little patience for others who aren't.

- *Indecision* — If someone comes to you with a question, you make a decision right on the spot. Decisions come easy for you. You expect the same from others and become frustrated when others can't make up their minds. You lose patience with people who respond, "I don't care," when asked what they would like to do.

- *Convention* — You don't enjoy the status quo. You don't have a "meat loaf" night at your house. You like to have something different every week. And you don't want to hear, "But that's the way we always do it."

Turn-Offs for the E

For Es everything is black and white. They believe everyone needs to pull his weight, and they become frustrated if someone doesn't. Es don't like to show emotion. They believe emotions are private and should be kept that way. They would never dream of telling a co-worker if they were having problems at home.

- *Ambiguity* — You like things to be clear. You want to make sure that there is no room for error. If your boss gives you a project and tells you to have it done next week, you will pin him down to an exact date.

- *Irreverence* — You don't like to hear anyone bad-mouthing the company. You are loyal, and you expect others to be also.

- *Laziness* — You are goal-oriented. You have a lot to accomplish, and you feel there is no room for slackers.

- *Showing Emotions* — You feel uncomfortable with others who act emotionally — crying, shouting, etc. You don't express your emotions openly, and you prefer that others keep theirs private also.

Turn-Offs for the L

Ls are caring, devoted people. In some respects, they view the world through rose-colored glasses. They expect everyone to feel as strongly about others as they do.

- *Insensitivity* — You are sensitive and caring, and you can't understand why everyone doesn't feel the same way.

- *Dissension* — You want everybody to be happy. You like to see people work together. When there is a conflict, you tend to step in and try to settle it.

- *Insincerity* — You enjoy receiving compliments, but not insincere ones. You are a good judge of character, and you can tell when people really mean what they say.

- *Egotism* — Because you are such a team player, you see no place for egotism. You believe the only way to be successful is to work together.

Turn-Offs for the F

In some respects Fs are loners. They don't appreciate it when others try to pull them in and make them part of the group.

- *Over-assertiveness* — Just because you are reserved doesn't mean you don't know what you are doing. You resent people who try to come in and tell you how to do something.

- *Carelessness* — You hold high standards for yourself as well as for others. You see no excuse for carelessness. You believe if people just take their time, they can do the job right.

- *Arrogance* — You dislike it when others act as if they believe they are better than you are. You believe you are just as capable as they are; you just don't advertise it.

- *Fakes* — You are good at what you do. You can spot a fake a mile away.

Conclusion

We all have likes and dislikes. Knowing what turns you on and turns you off can help you if you decide to look for a new job. For example, if you are an E who likes control, you wouldn't last a day at a job where you were given orders all day. Or if you were an L, you wouldn't last a day with a company full of Es who are totally bottom-line oriented and have no sensitivity.

Learning about the likes and dislikes of the various dimensions can help you in working with others. For example, if you are working with an S, you know he doesn't like to wait. If you plan a meeting with him, make sure you are on time. Or if you are working with an F, you know he requires lots of information. Don't ask him to prepare a report for the board. Give him a detailed memo outlining everything you expect him to include in the report.

6 IDENTIFYING THE STYLES OF OTHERS

By studying the various characteristics of the four styles, it's easy to identify the styles of others, even if they don't take the SELF Profile. Knowing what style a co-worker or friend is will help you in dealing more effectively with her.

For example, when your friend Cindy comes to town for a visit, she immediately moves in and takes over. You are an S, so a week's worth of mail is sitting on the countertop. Your family room looks like a bomb exploded. Within 24 hours, however, you catch Cindy organizing your papers. The next thing you know, she asks for a dust cloth and begins to dust your furniture. If you realize that Cindy behaves this way because she is an E personality who likes to get things organized, you probably will be able to accept her actions. If you don't, however, you are liable to resent her taking control of your life.

Following are some tips to help you identify the styles of friends and co-workers:

The S

When you walk into the office of an S, you may be shocked. Paper is stacked everywhere. Yet if you ask an S for a particular report, she will pick it out of the pile in a matter of seconds. Although there will be some pictures of family displayed, the office walls will be covered with plaques. You're also likely to see autographed photos of the S with famous people.

Ss are often flamboyant in their dress. Being risk takers, they will pull together outfits that others wouldn't dream of putting together — and they will look good.

Ss are full of energy. You probably won't see them sitting still — at least not for long. They read their mail or comb their hair while waiting at stoplights. They are in perpetual motion.

Change is important to Ss. They probably rearrange the furniture in their home and office on a regular basis.

The E

For the most part, the office of an E will be well-organized, although there may be some semblances of chaos. Es like to have charts on the wall so that they can follow their progress. Although almost everyone has DayTimers these days, Es use theirs to the fullest. They can't make a move without it.

Es tend to dress conservatively. They are traditionalists. They don't see a need to change something that has worked in the past. They have few, if any, pictures of their family in their office. They will probably have a few, but not too many, plaques and awards displayed.

The homes of Es are well-organized. They have a shopping list on the refrigerator and a calendar listing every activity that involves the family. Their shelves are neatly organized. In their family room, you may even find their CDs in alphabetical order.

The L

For the most part, the office of an L will also be well-organized, but there will be some half-finished projects sitting around. (Remember, the L will drop what she is doing at a moment's notice to help a co-worker.)

The offices of Ls tend to be comfortable. There are lots of pictures of the family displayed, drawings done by their children and plants from home. In the right-hand drawer of their desk you will find hot chocolate, hand lotion and aspirin.

You might also see employees going in and out of an L's office regularly. After all, the L is the one person who will sit and listen to everyone else's problems.

When a co-worker suffers a death in the family or retires, the L will be the one taking up a collection and asking everyone to sign a card. They are the ones who suggest that the company have a picnic and encourage others to get together outside the office.

The F

When you walk into the office of an F you know it right away. There are file cabinets lining the walls, labeled binders on the shelves and charts on the wall. If you look carefully at the charts, you will notice that they have been neatly done and have been placed perfectly on the wall. The office of the F is meticulously neat.

Fs also tend to dress conservatively. They are not risk-takers, so if it's between the dark blue suit that they know looks good or the gray one that is a little more flamboyant, they'll choose the blue suit every time.

The F's home is well-organized. It is tastefully decorated, but conservative. The F is practical and exacting. When preparing meals, he will stick with tried and true recipes and follow the instructions to a tee. When selecting a new car, she will buy the brand she has always bought. There's no sense in trying something he is unsure of.

Identifying the Different Personality Types in Your Office

To help you identify the different personality types in your office, read the following descriptions and see if you can identify which is the S, E, L and F.

Ann is the nurse manager at Memorial Hospital. She maintains an open-door policy and encourages her staff to come in and talk whenever they need to. In fact, she often spends a good deal of her day talking with her staff and the patients. Paperwork is always the last thing she does, and she often must take it home to complete it.

Ann considers her staff a team. They have daily meetings to discuss how the patients are doing. Every year at Christmas she invites her entire staff to her home for a holiday party.

Although Ann's office is small, it is warm and inviting. She has a coffee pot with extra mugs and a jar of candy on her desk. A big rubber tree plant sits in the corner, and next to it on the credenza is a picture of her husband and children.

Ann's infectious laugh makes everyone marvel at how she can be so "up" all the time. In reality, however, she is frustrated with the administration at the hospital. Sometimes she thinks maybe it's time to move on, but she likes the people she works with and feels that her staff and the patients need her.

Ann is an _____ personality.

Bob is an account representative for a public relations firm. He has a good working relationship with his clients and the people outside the office with whom he must work. He won't hesitate to call a reporter to pitch a story idea. He is confident of his skills and has developed personal friendships with many reporters.

Bob's clients trust him. He seldom has a client turn down a proposal he makes for a public relations or marketing campaign. Occasionally, he is too direct and has, on a couple of occasions, made clients angry. For example, Bob is quick to make decisions. One client asked him, "But wouldn't it be better if we did it this way?" Bob's answer was immediate and sharp. "No way," he said, "that would never work." The client asked to be assigned to another account representative.

Bob has lots of friends and enjoys going out. He is at his best in a social situation, and he often finds new clients on the golf course, at service club meetings or even at a ball game.

Even though most people think Bob has it all, deep down inside he worries about losing his social image. He works hard to keep his job because he believes a lot of his self-worth is tied to his position.

Bob is an _____ personality.

Larry is a researcher for an insurance organization. His office is in the library and his job is to research whatever issues he is assigned. He spends the entire day either behind his computer or poring over the manuals in his office or the library.

Larry works on one project at a time. He refuses to be rushed. He never turns in an assignment until he is absolutely sure the information is 100 percent correct.

When his co-workers ask Larry to go to lunch with them, he always turns them down. He prefers to eat a sandwich in his office alone while reading the latest journal.

Everyone in the office knows that if they have a question about anything, Larry is the one to go to. But Larry often gets annoyed when they walk into his office and ask him a question when he is in the middle of another research project.

Lately, Larry's boss has been telling him that he is taking too long to get projects finished. Larry is annoyed with his boss's attitude — he can't believe he wants him to rush through things that Larry feels are important. Larry's wife is also becoming annoyed. Larry is putting in more and more time at the office, and when he is home, he has his nose buried in work that he brought home from the office.

Larry is an _____ personality.

Margaret is the sales manager of the telephone sales department of a telecommunications company. She sets goals for her department on a regular basis. She has never missed a day's work since she started working for the company five years ago.

Behind her back, Margaret's staff laughs about her "uniform." Margaret wears a dark blue or black suit to the office daily. Many of her staff don't really care to work for her because they consider her to be overly critical. If one of her staff suggests doing something a different way, she immediately snaps and says, "No."

Margaret takes her monthly quotas seriously. She develops action plans to ensure that they are reached. If her staff doesn't achieve their quotas, she pushes them even harder the next month.

Margaret wants to become sales manager of the division. She has made it clear to her staff that is her goal and that no one will get in her way. She tells her staff, "If you can't carry your load, leave now." Margaret's department has a great deal of turnover. Because Margaret's department always reaches its goals, her boss can't figure out the problem.

Margaret is an _____ personality.

Now, list four co-workers whom you work with on a regular basis. Beside each write down his or her style.

_____   _____

_____   _____

_____   _____

_____   _____

Finding the Right Combination of Styles

To have a truly successful working atmosphere, it is important to have a combination of all four types of personalities. Typically, there are more Ls and Fs. This is common because the Ss and Es are the noise makers — they make all the waves. The Ls and Fs, on the other hand, tend to mind their own business and go with the flow. If there were more Ss and Es than Ls and Fs, nothing would get accomplished.

The information you learned in Chapter 5 — the likes and dislikes of the four styles — will help you interact more effectively with the people you work with. For example, now that you know that Fs like autonomy, you would never think of asking an F to lead a task force. Or knowing High Es prefer to work at a fast pace, you would not pair them with Fs, who prefer to take things slowly.

Should a group of employees working on a project together be the same type? Never! If they are, they'll never get the project done. The Ss will have a good time talking about the project and will probably go out together for lunch, but they will never get anything accomplished. The Es will spend the entire time arguing about the best way to do it. A group of Ls won't be able to make up their minds which way to do it and will be busy asking each other what they want to do. The Fs will spend all of their time researching the best way to do the project.

When putting together a team, ask an E to lead the group. Then make sure that there is an F who can do the research, an S who can keep things moving and an L who can help negotiate compromises when disagreements arise.

Conclusion

Knowing the characteristics of the four styles makes it easier to identify the styles of others. Armed with this information, you will be better able to interact with both friends and co-workers.

In the following chapters you will learn how you can work more effectively with the various styles.

Answers to Identifying Different Personality Types:

Ann is an L.

Bob is an S.

Larry is an F.

Margaret is an E.

7 USING THE SELF PROFILE TO WORK MORE EFFECTIVELY WITH OTHERS

Just as you are most comfortable working in a job that best matches your style, the same is true of the people you work with. Whether employee or boss, you can use what you have learned through the SELF Profile to make others feel more psychologically safe.

In Chapter 5 you learned some of the likes and dislikes of the various styles. In this chapter you will learn some of the positive actions you can take to enhance your working relationships with others and some of the actions you should avoid.

Positive Actions to Take When Working With an S

- *Show energy and enthusiasm.* If you have been assigned to work on a project with an S, let him know that you are excited about the project and about working with him. If you approach him with the attitude that you are working with him only because you have to and you'd rather do it yourself, you'll probably end up doing it yourself.

- *Show interest in what they are doing or saying.* Ss love recognition. Make an effort to listen intently to what they are saying. If an S wins an award through his professional organization, be sure to let him know that you are aware of it and congratulate him.

- *Allow Ss to be spontaneous.* Be careful not to be too structured with an S. You will get much better results if you hand an S a project, tell him what you want and then let him decide how to do it. Don't outline every detail of how you want the project done. Ss are creative; let them use that skill.

- *Yield to their need for attention and recognition.* With the S you can't say, "Good job," often enough. Above everything else, they like to feel that they are appreciated.

- *Try to agree with them as often as possible.* If you are working with an S on a project, give him encouragement, and he will work like crazy. For example, if he makes a suggestion don't ever say, "That won't work." Instead say, "You know, that's a good point. But I think if we make this one minor change, we can do it even better."

Positive Actions to Take When Working With an E

- *Show respect for an E's position and accomplishments.* Es like to be in control. Don't try to usurp their power. If you do, they are likely to put you in your place.

- *Plan on doing most of the talking.* Es are not people-oriented. Regardless of the job, they concentrate on the bottom line.

- *Yield to their need to be in control.* Whenever possible, give the E some control. For example, if you have an E working for you, occasionally put him in charge of a project or a section of the department.

- *Avoid disagreements in areas of common expertise.* Es have a need to be right. You will never win if you get into a discussion with them about a topic in which they feel they are experts. For example, if your brother-in-law is an avid football fan and you have definite ideas about why the team lost last Sunday, avoid discussing them with him.

- *Engage in activities that don't require much verbal interaction.* If you have friends or family members who are Es, they probably enjoy going to a movie with you or attending a sporting event. If you have an E co-worker, he would prefer a written memo rather than a personal telephone call. If you have E-Mail at your office, use it with the Es instead of the telephone.

Positive Actions to Take When Working With an L

- *Show sincere interest in Ls as individuals.* If you have an L co-worker, ask about his kids. If he comes to work and seems down, ask if there is anything he would like to talk about. Ls work better in an atmosphere where they feel that the employer respects them as individuals.

- *Listen; be caring and sensitive.* If an L walks in and tells you his mother just died, express sympathy and ask what you can do. Don't start the conversation by asking, "Does that mean I'll have to find someone else to finish the project you're working on?"

- *Be expressive.* An L would much rather hear, "This is a really fine piece of work you have created," as opposed to a simple "Good job."

- *Be casual and informal.* Ls feel most comfortable in a relaxed environment. Avoid having them make appointments to see you.

- *Converse.* Do your part to maintain the conversation. Ls are good listeners. In fact, they enjoy being helpful and feel good when you share your problems and concerns with them.

Positive Actions to Take When Working With an F

- *Listen carefully.* Fs tend to be reserved. In a discussion with an F, you need to listen carefully. Ask him specific questions. He may not bother to speak out unless you give him a clear opening.

- *Be friendly, unassuming and entertaining.* When dealing with an F, be friendly but don't push too hard to be friends. Remember, Fs are thorough. They will need to get to know you well before they will be comfortable being friends.

- *Be low-key and supportive.* Unlike an S, who needs to be approached with energy and enthusiasm, the F will respond more readily to a low-key approach. If you come on too strong, you are likely to overwhelm an F.

- *Be the initiator.* Since Fs don't like risks, they are not going to approach you with a good idea. However, if you think they have a good one, approach them and encourage them to tell you about it.

- *Ask their opinion.* Even though Fs tend to be quiet, they do like to express their opinions and will do so when asked. For example, if you are serving on a task force to develop a marketing strategy you might say, "John, you have done a great deal of research on this product. Do you have any ideas on how we might market it?"

Actions to Avoid

Just as there are actions you can take to motivate an individual in each dimension, there are also actions you should avoid when dealing with the various personality types.

Actions to Avoid When Dealing With an S

- *Avoid boring them.* Ss bore easily. For example, if you are leading a meeting with Ss, keep it moving. If you keep going back over the same material, they will eventually lose interest and tune you out.

- *Avoid being indifferent.* Ss like decision. If your subordinate comes to you and says, "Which way would you prefer to do this?" don't say, "I don't care," or "It doesn't matter." Even if you don't have a preference, choose one.

- *Don't let them bowl you over with energy.* Ss are full of energy. Don't be overwhelmed by them and react negatively to their ideas. If you do, they will get the impression that you are indifferent and lose enthusiasm.

- *Don't forget an S's birthday or other special occasions.* Ss like to be recognized. Birthdays and anniversaries are important to them. A simple "Happy birthday," or "Congratulations! I can't believe you've been working here five years!" will go a long way.

Actions to Avoid When Dealing With an E

- *Don't expect a lot of warm emotions.* Es are bottom-line oriented. If you tell them your dog died or your child is sick, chances are they will probably either quickly say, "I am sorry," and then talk about work, or they may not even respond.

- *Don't expect praise or thanks.* Es don't have a need for recognition, so they can't understand why others do. Don't be insulted if they don't thank you or if they don't praise your work.

- *Don't expound on your differences.* If you don't agree with an E on a particular subject, let it go, or avoid the subject all together, if possible.

- *Don't be offended if they are distant.* Because they are so goal-oriented, Es can appear to be distant and unapproachable.

Actions to Avoid When Dealing With an L

- *Avoid taking advantage of their willingness to help.* Ls are sensitive and helpful. You need to be careful, however, not to take advantage of their helpfulness. They like to have favors returned.

- *Avoid being distant and unapproachable.* Ls love people, and they are sensitive. If you come across as standoffish, the L will probably think he has done something to offend you.

- *Avoid being unappreciative or forgetting their efforts.* Ls will work hard for you. The greatest reward they can receive for their efforts is to have you tell them that they have done a good job. Example: Mary and her boss Chuck were not getting along well. Mary felt like Chuck was piling more work on her than anyone else. One day Chuck walked in and sat across from her desk and said, "Have I ever told you how much I appreciate all you do for this department?" "No, you haven't," Mary replied. "Well I do," Chuck said. "You are the only person in this department I can depend on." Suddenly Mary no longer felt dumped on; she felt like an integral part of the department.

- *Don't forget to return their favors.* Ls like to do nice things for people, but, by the same token, they like to have those favors returned. If the L co-worker helps you out on a project today, make sure you offer to help him the next time he is in a jam.

Actions to Avoid When Dealing With an F

- *Avoid being arrogant or boastful.* Fs are reserved. They are turned off by people who come on too strong or who act like they know it all. Fs often have a great deal of knowledge and know when someone is faking it.

- *Avoid being loud or pushy.* It's not in the nature of an F to be loud or pushy; therefore, they don't respond to other people who are.

- *If you don't know about something, don't act like you do.* Don't be a know-it-all around an F. Fs often know the answer. If they catch you acting like you know something when you really don't, they will lose trust in you.

- *Don't take over.* Because of their nature, Fs will probably allow you to step in and take over; however, inside they will resent it, and you will get little cooperation from them.

Conclusion

By learning what the four styles consider to be turn-ons and turn-offs, you can develop better working relationships with the people in your office. In this chapter, you learned about actions you can take to motivate others and actions which you should avoid.

8 SUCCESSFUL WORKING STRATEGIES

How you respond to a co-worker depends a great deal on whether she is a subordinate or peer or your boss. If you have subordinates who are Es, you will approach them differently than you would an E supervisor or manager. For example, if you have a subordinate who has E preferences, you can enhance your working relationship with her by giving her some control whenever possible. If you have a boss who is an E, she is unquestionably in control. Understanding her need for control, you do not question her authority, as this might jeopardize your relationship.

Following are some tips for creating positive working relationships with a subordinate or peer:

The S

- *Allow an S the flexibility to be creative.* Ss tend to be creative and enjoy using their creativity in their jobs. Whenever possible, allow them that flexibility. Be careful not to stifle their energy by demanding their conformity. Ss hate to hear, "But we've always done it that way."

- *Reward an S's efforts with your enthusiasm.* When the S turns in a report, don't say, "I'm sure it will be fine. I'll look it over later." Instead, say, "This really looks good. I can tell you put a lot of time into it. I'll look it over and let you know if I have any questions."

- *Channel their energy in appropriate directions.* This may be easier said than done. The Ss often have so much energy that it may be difficult to find enough interesting and exciting projects to keep them interested. Remember, Ss are risk-takers, so they may be perfect to take on a new project or explore an untried area.

- *Make sure Ss get lots of credit.* If an S was responsible for completing a project, make sure that the boss and other appropriate people know what part she took in the project.

- *Respect their need for socializing.* Don't become frustrated if you see them standing around the coffee pot chatting with co-workers or spending extra time at lunch. Ss have a strong need to socialize, and it is possible that they are spending their time talking with co-workers about work.

- *Don't forget to show them your appreciation for their new and thoughtful ideas.* Encourage their creativity by thanking them when they come up with new and unique ways of doing things. For example, "Thanks, Sally, for planning the office picnic. Everyone seemed to enjoy going to the amusement park this year instead of the city park."

- *Remember their motivations.* Ss tend to be unconventional. They are motivated by opportunities and friendship.

The E

- *Give Es the reins whenever possible.* Es need control. Take advantage of their efficient, practical, ambitious nature when you can. For example, if you ask two Es to work on a project together, it might be best to divide the project and ask each to be in charge of a specific aspect of it.

- *Take advantage of their need to clear up messes.* Es are organized. Whether it's the office storeroom or lagging sales, they are the best people to provide structure and get others back on track.

- ***Show respect for their traditional values and ways of thinking.*** Es tend to be traditionalists. Although you may have problems getting them to look at new ways of doing things, it is important to show them how much you appreciate their strong values. For example, James works as a writer in the corporate communications division of his business. Ever since he has been in communications, he has used a typewriter to create his work. His boss is trying to get him to change to a personal computer. A good way to approach him would be, "Jim, you've created some really excellent work on your typewriter over the years. I bet if you really put your mind to it, you could do the same on your personal computer."

- ***Work with Es to be more accepting of other methods of accomplishment.*** Es don't like change. They prefer tried and true methods. Try bringing them around slowly. For example, with Jim you might say, "You mentioned that your typewriter needs a good cleaning. Why don't you send it out this week and try writing next week's articles using the computer?"

- ***Don't get into their territory.*** Because they like control, Es don't appreciate your stepping into their territory, even if you think you are doing them a favor. For example, Leslie, an E, has been Bill's secretary for the past 10 years. Over the years he has given her an increasing amount of authority. Recently, a new secretary, Betty, joined the staff. Bill approached Betty and asked where Leslie was. Betty said that Leslie was out to lunch and asked if there was anything she could do. Bill gave Betty a letter to type. When Leslie returned and heard what had happened, she was furious. Leslie felt that Betty had taken on work that belonged to Leslie alone.

- ***Don't be passive.*** Es are very direct. They can't understand someone who can't get to the point. If you have an opinion, don't sit back and wait for an E to ask you what it is. Express yourself right up front.

The L

- *Use the peacemaking skills of an L to your advantage.* If you are having problems with a boss or co-worker, ask an L for her advice. Ls are good listeners and might be able to give you some new insights on how to make peace with the other person.

- *Treat them fairly, supportively and openly.* Ls live by the creed, "Do unto others …" They are fair, open and honest and expect to be treated the same way.

- *Allow them opportunities to interact with others.* Ls are social beings. Whenever possible, put them in positions where they can work with others.

- *Appeal to an L's principles and values.* For example, "I know you feel strongly about this issue, Mary. That's why I think you would be the best person to take on this project."

- *Avoid being harsh or insensitive.* When something happens in their family, Ls want to talk about it. Give them the opportunity to express how they feel. If you don't, you will seem harsh or insensitive.

- *Always acknowledge Ls when you pass them in the hall.* If you forget to say "hello" when you see them, they are liable to think that you are actually angry with them for some reason. They do tend to take everything personally.

- *Avoid harsh criticism.* If you say to the L, "This report is not what I wanted," they will take it as a personal remark. When dealing with an L, say, "I don't think I made it clear what I wanted. Let's sit down and talk."

The F

- *Listen carefully to what Fs have to say.* Fs may not be the boldest people in the office or the first to present ideas, but be assured they do have a lot of great ones. Just ask them, and then listen patiently.

- *Work with them to set deadlines.* Fs often have a difficult time meeting deadlines, not because they are irresponsible, but because they feel like the project is never good enough. Help them by setting deadlines and insisting that they adhere to them.

- *Give them space to operate.* Fs don't like people looking over their shoulders; they prefer to work alone. Give them an assignment and a deadline, and then let them do the job.

- *Pay attention to and appreciate their need for substance and credibility.* Fs have extremely high standards. This is important to them. If you are an S working on a project with an F, you may think that she is being too picky. Just remember, the F will make sure that your project doesn't fail because of inaccuracies.

- *Recognize that they are practical.* If you're looking for something different and creative, don't go to an F. They are much too practical. But if you want an idea that will work, an F is the person to ask.

- *Don't pressure them into forgoing their careful, exacting nature.* Remember, it's these traits that keep the rest of us honest. Asking them to do something in a hurry goes against their nature. Give them as much time as you possibly can.

- *Don't expect them to empathize in a crisis.* Unlike Ls, the Fs are much too practical to be emotional. If an employee unexpectedly dies, an F will not stand around talking about what a tragedy it was. They will probably ask if anyone has thought to set up a trust fund for the employee's children. The F won't take the initiative to do it, but that will be her first thought.

Tips on Working Successfully With a Supervisor/Manager

If you have ever had a personality clash with your boss, you know who eventually ends up winning. But you don't have to clash with your supervisor or manager. Using what you learned through the SELF Profile, you can create a more positive working relationship with your boss.

Following are some tips for working with bosses of the various dimensions:

The S

- *Be sociable.* Even if you are an all-business type person, try being sociable with your boss. You don't have to go out with her for dinner, but she will appreciate it if you ask her about her spouse and children. High Ss usually have pictures of their families in their office, so that provides the perfect opening.

- *Be flexible, open and spontaneous.* If your S boss asks you to change lunch hours or asks you to go to lunch with her on the spur of the moment, do it. You will show her that you can be flexible and spontaneous.

- *Show enthusiasm and excitement.* The High S boss is excited about her job, so she expects you to be excited about yours too. If you don't show any enthusiasm, she may view you as uncooperative.

- *Let her take the credit.* Remember, Ss like attention. If your boss says, "You put a lot of time in on getting this report done," respond by saying, "Yes, but you gave me the direction I needed to get it done right." If you do, you will be a winner.

- *Help her with organization.* If you are a secretary for an S personality, you have a big job ahead of you. Organization is not her strength. If you can help her get organized and stay organized, she will be grateful and will give you additional responsibility.

- ***Don't openly argue.*** Ss are extremely self-confident. Avoid arguing with them.

- ***Don't present just one conclusion.*** An S doesn't want to hear, "But that won't work." Instead say, "I don't believe that will work, but what if we try it this way," or "Here are several options we might consider."

- ***Don't use a win/lose approach.*** Ss are extremely competitive. Don't present things to them as win or lose. For example, don't ever say to a High S boss, "If I don't get that promotion, I will quit." If you do, your boss is likely to say, "I'm sorry you feel that way. I hope you can find another job where you will be happy."

The E

- ***Recognize that they are motivated by challenge.*** If your E boss gives you a quota that you are sure you can beat, suggest a higher one. Then challenge her to help you achieve it.

- ***Play by their rules.*** Es like control. When they are in charge, there is no doubt who will run the show. If you want to remain employed, don't rock the boat or question their authority.

- ***Be punctual, to the point and oriented toward results.*** If you have an E boss, make every effort to be on time. When you meet with her, make sure you know exactly what you are going to say. For example, "Ms. Smith, I just wanted to update you on my progress. I have completed the mailings to the first three mailing lists and will complete the fourth one tomorrow."

- ***Show that you are keenly aware of their authority.*** Unless you are told otherwise, always address the E boss by Mr. or Ms. They demand respect.

- ***Document everything with an emphasis on results.*** Don't ever go to an E boss and say, "We need to hire two more salespeople because our current staff is overworked." Instead say, "If we hire two additional salespeople we can increase our sales by 10 percent."

- *Be careful not to exhibit behaviors that an E may misinterpret as laziness.* For example, Sue enjoys reading the newspaper in the mornings. She often leaves her house early to avoid traffic, and then sits at her desk reading the paper until 8:30 a.m. — the official time that the office opens. If her boss is an E, she may be wondering why Sue isn't spending her extra time in the morning catching up on her work.

- *Don't expect more than a business relationship.* If you have an E boss you probably won't hear much about her family or her personal life. Because she is task-oriented, she believes employees have no business discussing personal business at work. Don't mention your family either.

- *Don't waste time chatting.* If you do, she'll just tune you out. When you meet with an E, get to the point.

- *Don't expect any strokes.* Es don't need strokes, so they don't believe others do either. Es are motivated by the job, not people. If your E boss doesn't tell you that you did a good job, it is not a reflection on your performance. It is just her communication style.

The L

- *Openly express your thoughts, concerns and ideas.* Remember, Ls are good listeners. If you are concerned about the progress of a job, discuss your concerns with your boss. If you have a good idea, share it with her. She will love to hear it and will probably ask you to tell her more.

- *Be a team player.* Ls are extremely team-oriented. You can win the respect of an L if you make it clear that you want to be a part of her team.

- *Show interest in your supervisor/manager as a person.* Like Ss, Ls don't mind having their personal lives brought into the workplace. If you know your boss's mother or father has been ill, ask about them on a regular basis. Your boss will appreciate your concern.

- *Make it easy for them when they have to be directive.* Since Ls don't have a particularly high need to control, they often don't feel comfortable when thrown into highly authoritative positions. If your boss suddenly finds herself in charge of a group of people, be supportive of her actions.

- *Set your own performance goals and then make sure you achieve them.* Since Ls are so people-oriented, they sometimes have a difficult time setting work goals. You may need to set your own and follow through.

- *Don't take advantage of their good nature.* Generally, Ls are good-natured. Even though it might be tempting, don't take advantage of this trait. For example, if you know that asking your boss if you may leave early will leave her in a bind, don't ask.

- *Don't forget the importance of social rapport and informal chats.* If your boss asks you to lunch or suggests going out after work, do it. It will give you a great opportunity to get to know her better.

- *Don't forget to listen and be patient.* Ls are good listeners but they also like to be listened to. When they are talking, never interrupt.

The F

- *Acknowledge their expertise.* Fs are good at what they do. If you have an F boss, let her know how much you appreciate her expertise. For example, "I'm so glad to have the opportunity to work with you, Leslie. I know that I will learn a lot from you."

- *Give facts, data and be consistent.* If your F boss asks you to gather information on a competitor's product, make sure you are thorough. Be sure to get all the facts and then present them in an organized, clear way.

- *Think things through and document ideas with facts from credible sources.* Never say to the F boss, "I just think we should do it this way," without explaining why.

- *Offer detailed, well-thought-out plans of action.* Don't throw a proposal for your boss together. Instead, research it carefully, and then present it with a detailed action plan. For example, "In order to meet our quota, I intend to take the following steps."

- *Present fresh, new approaches.* Fs have a difficult time coming up with new approaches to doing things. They are not risk-takers and prefer the status quo. They enjoy hearing new ideas. However, be careful to document and detail every aspect of what you plan.

- *Do your homework.* Don't present a half-baked idea to your boss. Fs know immediately whether or not something has been carefully researched. When dealing with the F, do your homework and have the facts. If you do, you will gain her respect.

- *Don't be in a hurry to prove yourself or push through your new ideas.* Fs have high standards. They need to have things proven to them. Proceed cautiously.

- *Don't appear arrogant or cocky.* F bosses want to see results, not hear self-imposed praise. They believe actions speak louder than words.

- *Don't expect high risk or surprise in decision-making.* Unless forced to by upper management, the F boss will probably do things according to the status quo.

Conclusion

By trying to adapt to the working styles of others, you can help them feel more psychologically comfortable with you. Just as certain actions make you more comfortable, the same is true of your boss and co-workers. By flexing your style slightly, you can improve your working relationship with even the most difficult person.

9 USING THE SELF PROFILE IN CONFLICT RESOLUTION

When a conflict arises between two individuals, it normally is caused by a lack of communication or a lack of understanding of the other person's feelings. Conflict is seldom the result of two people who just want to be difficult.

Let's look at Mary and Fred, who both work at Angels of Mercy Hospital. Mary is the nurse manager on the fifth floor. She is an E personality. Fred, an L, is a nurse and is responsible for 10 patients. Mary and Fred are constantly arguing. Mary says Fred is disorganized. He never seems to complete everything in the time he has. Fred, on the other hand, says Mary is too stilted and that she really doesn't care about the patients, only about her next promotion. Here is a typical conversation between Mary and Fred.

Mary: "Fred, have you explained to Mrs. Byers how to take care of her sutures after she goes home tomorrow?"

Fred: "Not yet. I'll do it this afternoon."

Mary: "You've had all morning to do it. Why isn't it done?"

Fred: "When I went to take Mr. Brooks's vital signs this morning, he was a little depressed, so I sat and talked with him. Did you know when he goes home there will be no one to take care of him?"

Mary: "That's not your job. If he is having problems, call social services or the chaplain. Just do your job."

Who's wrong? Actually neither Fred nor Mary is wrong. They both have the same goal — to take care of the patients in the best way possible. But, because of their different personalities, they don't agree on what the best way is.

As an E, Mary is more concerned with the task, not the people. She believes that nurses can't adequately do their jobs if they get too caught up in the lives of their patients. She is goal-oriented. When she starts the day, she has a list of everything that she and her staff need to accomplish. If it is not done, she feels as if she has failed.

Fred is a typical L. He's sensitive, helpful and a good listener. When he noticed that Mr. Brooks looked depressed, he couldn't just walk away. It's just not in his personality.

Does this mean that Mary and Fred will just continue to clash? It doesn't have to. If Mary and Fred use what they learn from their SELF Profiles, they will find that they can not only work without conflict, but can actually complement each other's styles. If you are faced with a similar situation, the following tips may help you overcome conflicts both at work and in your personal life.

Ask Yourself How You Are Contributing to the Situation

In most disagreements there is no clear-cut right or wrong. If you look closely, you will normally find that the other individual isn't purposely trying to be difficult: his style is just different from yours. When you find yourself in conflict with another, ask yourself, "What am I doing to contribute to this situation?"

Let's look at neighbors Brenda and Sue. Sue, an F, is retired. She spends most of her day taking care of her lawn and tending her flowers. She is meticulous. Her flowers could win awards. When fall comes, she begins to rake her leaves the minute they hit the ground.

Brenda and her husband, Bill, have three young children and live next door to Sue. Brenda and Bill moved into the neighborhood six months ago. Since that time Brenda, an S, has tried to make friends with Sue, but Sue doesn't seem interested. When Brenda's children are playing, they often run into Sue's yard. Sue hasn't said anything, but inside she is burning up. Yesterday, one of the children threw a ball into Sue's yard, and it landed in her flower bed. The children rushed in to retrieve it. Sue came tearing out of her house screaming, "Stay out of my flower bed, you little brats!"

Brenda can't believe Sue reacted that way. "What's the problem?" she snaps. "They're just flowers."

Using the tip just suggested, Brenda must first ask herself, "What am I doing to contribute to this situation?" Seeing Sue at work in her yard all the time should indicate to Brenda that Sue is meticulous about her flowers. A typical F, the perfection of the flowers is extremely important to her. Realizing this, Brenda could help the situation by apologizing to Sue and then making sure her children stay out of Sue's yard.

If Sue asked herself, "What am I doing to contribute to this situation?" she would probably have to answer, "I should have spoken up sooner and asked Brenda to keep the children out of my yard. I need to understand that accidents do happen."

Using the SELF Profile to Avoid Conflict

Personalities that criss-cross on the SELF Profile have the greatest difficulty understanding each other. That means that Fs and Ss tend to have more conflicts with each other and Es and Ls typically have more conflicts.

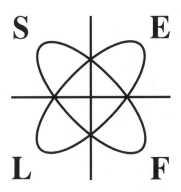

Does that mean that these individuals are bound to clash? Not necessarily. By being aware of the other people's personality profiles and their special needs, it's possible to lead a fairly harmonious life. Let's look first at Ss and Fs.

Ss have a laid-back, carefree attitude that Fs find hard to tolerate. To the freewheeling S, an F seems uptight and stuffy. Neighbors Sue and Brenda are perfect examples.

Sue looks at Brenda as being lazy and careless, but with Brenda and Bill both working, they are lucky if they have a chance to mow their grass once every two weeks, let alone plant flowers or trim the hedge.

Brenda, by the same token, can't understand why Sue isn't more sociable. She never has friends over and seldom goes out. "She's just a mean old lady," Brenda tells Bill. "But that's no reason to take it out on us and our kids."

If Brenda and Sue knew each other's SELF Profile, they would understand why they react the way they do and then would be more tolerant of each other. For example, Sue would see that Brenda isn't lazy, just a busy mother with three active children. As an S, Brenda just doesn't let things bother her; she is more relaxed than Sue. Just because her yard isn't perfectly kept doesn't mean that she is careless. Having a well-manicured lawn isn't at the top of her priority list.

By the same token, Brenda would see that Sue really isn't a mean old lady; she is just more reserved. She doesn't have a lot of friends because she prefers spending time alone. She was upset about the ball being thrown into her flower bed because she takes a great deal of pride in her flowers.

Es and Ls also often have a difficult time relating to each other. Let's examine the case of Bob and Larry. They have been assigned by their boss to plan the company Christmas party.

Bob is an L. Being team-oriented, Bob feels they should ask the others in the office what they would like to do. He suggests polling the other employees to see if they would rather have a catered luncheon in the office or a less extravagant buffet dinner in the evening with spouses.

Larry is an E. He is not married, so he thinks the idea of a dinner with spouses isn't necessary. When the two sit down to talk, here's what happens:

Bob: "Let's go ask the others what they would like."

Larry: "Nah. That would be a waste of time. Let's just have a lunch here; it would be a lot easier. Here is a list of caterers. Call them and get prices. We'll want to have turkey, ham, a cranberry salad, mashed potatoes and rolls."

Bob: "I don't agree. I don't think it's right for us to plan this without asking the others what they think."

Larry: "Oh, you're just sore because you want to bring your wife."

Bob: "I don't want to argue. We'll do it your way."

If Bob and Larry had taken the SELF Profile, chances are things would not have escalated to this point. Bob would have realized that Larry wanted the catered lunch because that was the easiest and quickest thing to do. He likes things to be fast-paced and organized. When he is given a project, he wants to jump right into it.

Larry, on the other hand, would have realized that Bob is not comfortable making decisions. Because he is team-oriented, he feels that it is important to get the opinions of others. He doesn't feel the need to jump right into things the way Larry does.

With this information, look how the conversation could have turned out.

Bob: "Let's go ask the others what they would like to do."

Larry: "I don't think it's necessary to ask everyone. How about talking to one person from each department? Meanwhile, I'll call some caterers and see what the difference in price would be between having a meal in the afternoon as opposed to the evening."

Bob: "Sounds good to me. Let's meet again after lunch and compare notes."

By doing it this way, both Bob and Larry feel good. Bob is able to get some other opinions which he feels is important, and Larry can jump right into the project by gathering information from the caterers.

If you understand your personality dimensions and know the strengths and weaknesses of the people around you, they won't seem nearly as difficult. The trick is to understand what you need to feel psychologically safe, and then ask for it.

On the other hand, realize that others also need to feel psychologically safe. By flexing your style, you will be more likely to meet their needs. It is a matter of respecting and valuing your differences. When you do, you will experience a lot less stress in your relationships with others in your life.

Three Ways to Resolve Conflict

Even when you understand your personality style and those of others, you still may occasionally find yourself in conflict. If you do, here are some tips to help you.

- *Mirror the other person's behavior.* Mirror the other person's posture and pacing for a more successful communication effort. For example, Greg and Rob have been asked to work on an advertising campaign together for the company's biggest client. Greg is an E and Rob is an F. When the two sit down together to develop the campaign, Greg immediately says, "I know how we should do this. We should center the ad around a Western theme."

  "Wait a minute," Rob says. "I think we need to do some market research first — find out who their customers are."

  "They sell jeans and flannel shirts — who do you think their customers are?" Greg snaps. Rob is immediately defensive, and in true F fashion, withdraws from the discussion.

  Instead of reacting, Greg can diffuse the situation by mirroring Rob's behavior. In other words, he can use some of the behaviors of an F. He may not want to move as cautiously as Rob, but if he slows down a little, they will relate better to each other.

How does mirroring help?

— It enables you to control the situation.

— You can defuse the explosiveness of the situation.

— You make the other person feel comfortable because he perceives you as being like he is.

- *Be a model.* If mirroring is too explosive and intense, model the behavior. Do this by validating the feelings of the angry person. For example, say, "I see that you are upset, but I would like to try to understand why. Let's sit down and relax for a moment, and then you can tell me what it is that is bothering you."

When modeling behavior, remember the following:

— *Remain calm.* If you remain calm, the other person will calm down also.

— *Don't get angry.* Regardless of how angry you are, don't show it. If you don't react with anger, the other person will not have a reason to remain angry.

— *Don't talk loudly.* If your voice is naturally loud, tone it down. If you don't, the other person is liable to misinterpret your tone and think you are upset and angry.

- *Be clear.* Just because the other person heard what you said doesn't necessarily mean that he understood you. Sometimes *intent* is different than *content*. For example, if you say, "I'll clean that up," you may simply mean that — you will take care of it. However, depending on how you say it, or how the other person interprets it, they may think you mean that you will clean it up because they won't or can't. If you tell the individual exactly what you mean, there is no room for misunderstanding. For example, "I'll clean that up since I've finished my job. Don't worry about it."

Easing Out of Difficult Situations

Even if you're not in a conflict with another individual, you may find that you are in a difficult situation. To ease out of difficult situations, consider the following techniques.

- *Make things objective.* Avoid the words "but," "yet" and "however." Using them negates the first part of your sentence. For example, if you say, "I see what you're saying. Let's explore the alternatives," it will sound more positive than "I see what you're saying, but let's explore the alternatives."

- *Tread water.* If you are so upset that you don't think you can be civil, tread water. Comment on something in the room. "Is that a picture of your family?" Use small talk to relieve the tension. "Wasn't that some game yesterday?"

- *Compliment your adversary and be sincere.* "With your knack for organization, I know this project will be a winner. Now let's talk a little more about the best way to go about completing it."

- *Try to help each other stay afloat instead of independently struggling.* Consider the advantages of working together. What can you do to strengthen each other? Concentrate on what you have in common. Focus on the mutual area of benefit. Ask yourself the following:

    — What's in it for both of us?

    — Do we share any common goals, needs or desires?

    — What do we need to do in order for both of us to get our needs met?

- *Clarify the end-result up front.* Figure out what you both want to gain. If your two needs conflict, negotiate and compromise until you each reach your goals.

- *Establish a comfort zone.* Using what you have learned from the SELF Profile, make the other person feel at ease.

Tips to Help You Avoid Clashes

Whenever two or more people work together, there are bound to be occasional clashes. The following tips will help you eliminate the unnecessary ones.

1. ***Become self aware.*** Mastering the SELF Profile will help you gain a better understanding of what you and others really want.

2. ***Care for others.*** You can reduce relationship tensions through negotiations. Say to the individual, "I'll give up some of my needs to meet your needs if you will do the same for me."

3. ***Slow down and listen.*** Step back and listen to what the person is saying and what they are not saying. With your knowledge of the SELF Profile, you should be able to filter their words through their different personality styles.

4. ***Remember, you're in control.*** You have control of your feelings. Nobody can make you angry. You allow yourself to feel angry.

5. ***Tell yourself you are great.*** You are great, and it doesn't hurt to reinforce that sentiment to yourself. If you make a mistake, admit it and move on. It's not the end of the world.

6. ***You can do it.*** Maintain your sense of self-confidence. Affirm your strengths and give yourself a boost.

7. ***Share.*** Share information with others. When you do, state your intent as well as your content. The more information others have, the more open they are to communication.

Conclusion

Don't let conflicts keep you from getting the job done. By using what you learned in the SELF Profile, you can keep the number of conflicts you have with others to a minimum.

When you find yourself in the midst of a conflict, start by asking yourself, "What am I doing to contribute to this situation?"

Realize that personalities that criss-cross on the SELF Profile often have difficulty understanding each other. Knowing that up front and understanding the differences will help limit your conflicts.

If you find yourself embroiled in conflict, remember the following: Mirror the other person's behavior; be a model and be calm.

10 USING THE SELF PROFILE TO MAKE A CAREER CHANGE

To be truly successful in your job, it's important that you work in a job that is a good fit with your personality style. If you don't, it's like putting a round peg in a square hole: you may be able to force it in, but it's never going to be a good fit.

For example, if you are an S, an individual who likes people and is socially skilled, you will not be comfortable in a job that allows no contact with other people. Not only will you be unhappy, but before long, your work will begin to suffer. On a personal level, working in a job that doesn't match your personality can prove stressful.

You may not be in the right job because you fell into the one you have. For example, Lisa agreed to go back to work after her youngest child started school. On the first day of school, her husband reminded her of her promise. Deep down inside Lisa believed no one would hire her. She had little training and even less experience. She planned to apply at three or four places, but she thought she would have to tell her husband that no one would hire her.

Lisa's first stop was at an insurance company. She applied for a data entry job. Much to her surprise, she got it. From 8 in the morning until 5 at night, other employees brought her what seemed like endless reams of paper. Her desk was never clear. Lisa was unhappy. After being at home where she made major decisions for her family, she now felt she had no control at her job with the insurance company. Unfortunately, Lisa felt she didn't have a choice: she had made a deal with her husband.

Lisa doesn't have to be unhappy. She believes the reason she is unhappy is that she really doesn't want to be at work. But, if Lisa examined the situation carefully, she would find that what she really doesn't like is her job. If Lisa found a job that better suited her style and situation, she would be happier.

Let's imagine that Lisa took the SELF Profile and pursued a job that fit her personality. An L, Lisa likes working with people. She enjoys helping resolve conflicts and using her organizational skills. With this information, Lisa finds the perfect job. She is the secretary at her children's school. She now feels close to her children, and she is able to use her people skills. As secretary, she has to deal with the principal, teachers, students and even parents. Occasionally, she even steps in to help mediate a conflict between students. You spend a good deal of time at work. When you get up in the morning, you need to look forward to going to work, and not dread it.

Helping Employees Make a Career Change

If you are a supervisor or manager, you may discover that you have employees who aren't a good fit for the job they have. You know they are not working out, and yet you hesitate to fire them. Sometimes, firing an individual who is not suited for a job is the best thing you can do: you are freeing them to find a job where they will be more comfortable.

If you find yourself in a position of having to fire an employee who just isn't working out, make sure she understands that it is not that she is the wrong person for the job, but that the job is wrong for her. Then, given what you learned through the SELF Profile, suggest some areas that might suit her better.

For example, Jim is a manager at a fast-food restaurant. Two weeks ago he hired Sally to work the counter. She is extremely slow in taking the orders and barely looks at the customers. Several customers, in fact, have complained to Jim that she has been rude.

Jim will eventually need to fire Sally. Sally, an F, would be better suited for a job where she didn't have to work with the public and where she could use her analytical skills. Perhaps she could find a job in accounting or computer systems.

When It's Time for You to Make a Change

Answer yes or no for each question. This test will help you determine if you are a candidate for burnout or if it's time for a career change.

1. When you're not at your job, in your spare time, do you get ideas that might help you with your job? _____

2. When you're talking to other people about your job, do you express the idea that you are only in it for the money? _____

3. Is TGIF (Thank God It's Friday) your favorite slogan, or do you long for the weekend and just hate Mondays? _____

4. Do you have talents you are not using at work, and are you complimented for these talents elsewhere? _____

5. When you socialize with people who are in the same line of work as you, are you usually comfortable? _____

6. Do you often say, "I wish I had become a _____"? (something different than what you currently are) _____

7. When it's time for an appraisal or your review, do you dread the meeting with your boss? _____

8. When you talk about your profession to other people who are new to it, do you say disparaging things like, "This is a crummy profession," or "You'll be sorry you're in it." _____

9. Think of the people with whom you associate most at work. Are they generally dissatisfied also? _____

10. When you think of your job, do you generally think of the hours you work and the perks you get rather than the important issues associated with your profession? _____

11. When you're with other people, do you find yourself talking about your job a great deal, probably more than they would like? Does your spouse say, "I wish you wouldn't talk about your job so much when we are out with our friends"? _____

Scoring the Job Change Quiz

Look at the 11 questions you just answered. If you answered "no" to the first and last question and "yes" to the rest, you are a good candidate for a job change. The more "yeses" you had for questions two through 10, the more you need to make a change. Before you quit your job, however, consider your choices. You do have choices. Consider all your options before making a move.

- *You can do nothing.* Although this may not seem like much of a choice, if you've made the decision that you need to move on and you don't, you've actually made a decision. This may not be the right time to get another job. For example, if you will be vested in the company's retirement plan in another six months, you may decide to stay, at least short-term.

  Before changing jobs, it's also important that you make sure that it's not your personal life that is causing your bad feelings about your job. Let's look at Ann. When Ann's youngest child entered school, she decided to return to the workforce. After months of searching, she found what she considered to be the perfect job. It was in her field of expertise, it paid more than she expected to make and she enjoys the work. She does, however, have to put in long hours.

  At home, Ann's husband is unhappy, and the children constantly complain. Ann no longer has time to cook the elaborate meals the family enjoyed. The house always seems to be messy, and she can't keep up with the laundry.

  Ann's problem is not the job; it's her personal life. No matter what job she gets, she will feel stressed. Ann must enlist more help and support from her children and husband. Once she gets her personal life in order, she may feel differently about her job.

- *Reinvigorate your job.* Take courses that relate to your area of work. Develop new skills or find new ways to do your job. Be creative. For example, Betty is the office manager for a company with approximately 20 employees. She is becoming bored with the routine chores she does on a daily basis. Recently, a flyer from the local Junior College came across her desk offering a course on creating newsletters. She approached her boss and asked if she could take the course and develop a monthly newsletter for the office.

- *Change jobs, but stay in the same field.* Maybe it's not the work that's the problem, but the people or the industry. Using the information you gained from the SELF Profile, investigate these possibilities.

  For example, John is an S. He thrives on change. He is currently employed as a technical writer. All day long he sits behind his computer and writes computer manuals. He has very little contact with people. As an S, John is creative and enjoys people. He might do better to work in the communications department of an organization where his job would entail interviewing employees and then writing feature articles for the firm's publications. Being socially skilled would also help him get information from many different kinds of people.

- *You can change careers.* If you learned through the SELF Profile that you are in the wrong job, it's time to change careers. If you are an F, you will probably feel uncomfortable with this idea since you do not enjoy taking risks. If you are an E, however, you may not be as hesitant. Remember, you can't grow without change. Although change may be uncomfortable, if you change jobs you will only be uncomfortable for a short period of time. If you choose to stay in the job you're in, you will be uncomfortable for a long time.

Consider Your Personal Working Strategies

As you learned through the SELF Profile, you have working strategies that best fit your personality type. If you decide to take a job, consider your own personal working strategies before making a move.

The S

Following are some adjectives that describe a typical S's working strategies:

- *Energetic*
- *Quick*
- *Enterprising*
- *Creative*
- *Enthusiastic*
- *Aware*
- *Stimulating*
- *People-person*

When choosing a job, be sure to find one that allows you to use all of these strategies. For example, if you are an S, you might enjoy a job in real estate, advertising or promotion or even starting your own company.

The E

If you are an E, you probably possess many of these qualities:

- *By the Book*
- *Bottom-line Oriented*
- *Administrative*
- *Impatient About Details*
- *Efficient*
- *Make Quick Decisions*
- *Organized*
- *Loyal*

As an E, you will do well in a management position. You are bottom-line oriented, and you enjoy directing others. You also enjoy jobs that allow you to use your organizational skills. You would probably like working as a sales manager or a manager of any department where you are guided by quotas.

The L

If you are an L, you enjoy working in companies where you can use the following working strategies:

- *Arbitrator*
- *Adaptive*
- *Flexible*
- *Compromising*

- *Fair*
- *Loyal*
- *Cooperative*
- *Helpful*

As an L, you enjoy working with others as a team. You would do well in a job where employees must work together to develop the final product. Because you enjoy conflict resolution and you are a good listener, you would make an excellent customer service representative.

The F

If you are an F, look for jobs that allow you to use the following working strategies.

- *Does Well in a Routine*
- *Data-Seeker*
- *Supports Structure*
- *Dependable*

- *Controlled*
- *Steady*
- *Conservative*
- *Organized*

Given these work strategies, you would enjoy working in a library, an engineering firm, an architectural firm or in research.

Examine Your Skills

Using the information you gained from your SELF Profile, examine your various skills.

- *People Skills.* Do you enjoy working with people? Can you successfully motivate others to get the job done? Generally, Ss and Ls like working with other people. An L might be an outstanding social worker. Ls are helpful, good listeners and arbitrators, all skills that would come in handy when dealing with their clients. Ss, on the other hand, would probably do well in a management position. They are socially skilled and can inspire others, which will help them motivate others to get the job done. Es and Fs are not as skilled in interpersonal relations.

- *Organizational Skills.* When it comes to organizational skills either you have them or you don't. Of all the styles, Es and Fs are the most organized. Not Ss — that's because they tend to be creative. They have many good ideas coming at them all at the same time, and they are trying to figure out a way to get them all done. Organization is not high on the L's list of priorities, either.

- *Research Skills.* Fs were made for jobs requiring research. Their analytical style is a definite plus. Ss often are not good researchers. They do not have the patience needed to do a thorough job.

- *Action Skills.* If you enjoy physical work, you will never feel comfortable if you have to sit behind a desk all day. You need to consider how active you like to be when you consider your job choices.

   Ss typically enjoy lots of action. For example, an S who is an emergency room nurse would probably have a hard time adjusting to working as a nurse in a doctor's office.

- *Creative Skills.* If you have creative skills, you will want to make sure you are in a job where you can use your creative abilities. Advertising, promotion, marketing and designing are obvious areas in which you would thrive.

Before making any kind of a move, either within your company or outside of your company, consider your skills and what you enjoy doing, and then make a list of the jobs that would be appropriate.

In addition to skills, you have to consider the various work classifications that are available. There are: skilled labor, business, economics, finance, health sciences, social sciences, math and physical science, communications and the arts. List these areas and then see where your skills match up best. For example, let's say that you are an E with a degree in math. You might consider being a math teacher or a comptroller.

Taking It Slow

If you really aren't certain about how you feel about your job, keep a journal for a month. Each day, write down how you feel about your job that day. You may find that you are unhappy because you are currently in the midst of a very trying project, but you actually like your job. Once the project is finished, you might be surprised to discover that you now feel okay about your job.

If, after a month, no reason surfaces for your unhappiness, begin to make plans to move. Think long and hard about your current job to help you determine what it is you don't like so you don't get into the same situation. Before starting your search, consider the following:

- *What do you dislike about your job?* Do you like or dislike working with people? Do you like or dislike doing routine tasks? Do you like or dislike doing detail work? Do you like or dislike sitting behind a desk all day?

- *What could you do without?* Could you work without supervision? If you currently have an office, could you accept a position where all you had was a desk in the corner? Do you need a certain amount of authority?

- *If you could do anything you want, what would it be?* Let your imagination go wild. Peter accepted a job right out of school working for the Post Office. He had just married his childhood sweetheart, and within two months they discovered a baby was on the way. Twenty-five years later, the kids are no longer living at home, and Peter is feeling dissatisfied with his job. At the Post Office, he is a clerk behind the counter. He admits he has never really enjoyed dealing with the public, and he would prefer to be working outside.

Peter could make a move within the Post Office — he could become a letter carrier or truck driver who delivers mail between stations — or he could leave the Post Office. Perhaps he also enjoys working with his hands and would like to get into a landscaping business or construction.

- *What are you looking for in terms of job satisfaction?*

Security. If you are an L or F, security will probably be important to you. You would function best in an established company that offers good benefits.

Peer Recognition. Ls need to feel like they are accepted. They get this through peer recognition. They would do well working in a company which recognizes the "Employee of the Month" or where employees are regularly praised for their work. Ss also need peer recognition. They need to feel appreciated. Es and Fs need people less. As far as they are concerned, it is the job that is important — not the people.

Structure. Es and Fs will function better in more structured environments. The Es, particularly, will do well in a job where they need to meet quotas regularly. Ss and Ls, on the other hand, thrive best where they have a little freedom. Ss, particularly, enjoy jobs where they can use their creativity. Neither Ss nor Ls would do well working in a factory where a whistle was blown indicating the beginning and ending of the workday.

To help you sort out what is most important to you, write each job need on a 3x5 card. Lay them out in front of you and ask yourself which ones are most important. Start with your top priority — the one that is absolutely essential — and then line them up accordingly. Then, as you consider the career options open to you, match them with your priority cards. Look for a job that matches your highest priorities in job needs.

Set Goals

Whatever you decide to do, set goals. In doing so, set realistic goals. If you set your goals too high, you will burn out, become discouraged and give up. If you set them too low, you will not be challenged to reach beyond where you already are.

Here are some rules for goal setting:

1. *Put your goals in writing.* By writing your goals you make them more specific. Also putting them in writing tends to make them more real.

2. *Be specific.* Don't just say, "I am going to continue my education." Be specific: "I will get my MBA within three years." That is something you can measure, and it gives you something to aim for. If you can't measure your goal, you will never know when you've reached it.

3. *Develop action plans.* For example:

   — I will take two courses per semester and one course during the summer.

   — In order to give myself more time to study, I will hire a cleaning service for the next three years.

   — I will pay for my schooling with my annual bonus.

   — I will make arrangements with my husband to take the children to their after-school activities on the nights I have class.

4. *Develop a timeline.*

5. *Understand that goals are not set in concrete.* Circumstances may cause you to eliminate or change your goals. For example, in the goal just mentioned, you may decide after the first semester that two classes per semester are too many. In that case, you may have to change your action plan to take only one class per semester.

Consider Who Else a Change Might Affect

If you have a family, you need to consider how such a move will affect your family. If you are the breadwinner and you decide to take a job earning half your current income, that will affect the way the family lives. That's not to say you can't do it, but you need to discuss it with the family ahead of time.

Changing jobs can also mean changes in life-style. For example, if you currently work from 9 a.m. to 3 p.m. and are home with your children before they go to school and when they get home, and you are considering a job where you have to leave by 7:30 a.m. and you won't get home until 5 p.m., you will need to negotiate a plan with the children or your husband.

Start by talking with your spouse. Then sit down with the children and say, "This is what I am thinking about doing. In order to do it, however, I am going to need your cooperation."

If you have been out of the workforce for a while, you must first determine if you need to go back to school. You may also find that this may not be the right time to go back to work full-time. If it's not, consider part-time or temporary work.

Keep looking until you find the right job. If you find yourself constantly changing jobs, however, you may be on the wrong track. Take the SELF Profile again and make sure that the jobs you are seeking match your personality type.

Conclusion

If you are unhappy in your job, it may be you are not suited for the job you have. If that's the case, you need to consider making a move. Before you do, however, do the following:

- *Consider your options*

- *Examine your working strategies*

- *Examine your skills*

- *Go slowly*

- *Set goals*

If you do all of these things, you won't have to worry about jumping into another job that you are not suited for.

11 SUMMARY

Now that you have completed the SELF Profile and know more about yourself and others, there are a few guidelines you should remember in using this information.

- The information in the SELF Profile is designed to aid you in self-awareness and in understanding others in broad and general terms. However, there will always be exceptions to these general categories. Human beings are complex creatures whose behaviors are greatly affected by a variety of factors. Therefore, they are not easily categorized.

- Always remember that an individual's behavior can be affected by the situation he is in. You can expect individuals to exhibit a variety of different characteristics depending on what is going on in their lives. The key is to look for consistent information across several settings before categorizing others into any one dimension.

- An individual's social style is the product of many years of development and is not easily changed. You will be wise to accept others as they are, with both their strengths and limitations, rather than try to change them.

- No one personality style is better than any other. Yet your social interactions with others can be greatly enhanced if you have an understanding of the motivations, strengths and weaknesses of both yourself and others. The SELF Profile is your tool for gathering such information.

One Last Look at the Styles

Working with the SELF Profile, you can learn to relate comfortably to a wide variety of people and feel confident of your communication skills. Your knowledge of the SELF Profile is an asset both on and off the job.

When dealing with the four different styles, remember the following:

The S

Ss are extremely expressive. They are motivated by recognition. They dislike routine and indecision. They are spontaneous. When an S goes shopping, he literally swoops through the stores. He spends no time debating over the wide striped tie or the thin striped tie: he knows immediately which he likes best. When things don't go well, Ss tend to blame others. They don't like accepting blame.

When choosing a career, Ss need to look for a job where they will have their ideas and achievements recognized. If they don't, they won't feel fulfilled. Their worst fear is losing their social image. Ss want others to recognize that they are successful.

The E

Es love success. The have little or no tolerance for laziness. They don't care for people who are irreverent about things the Es consider important, because they tend to be loyal, traditional people. Like Ss, they make quick decisions. They can also change their decisions as quickly as they make them and not look back. The enjoy positive strokes also, but they want their positive strokes to be for their accomplishments. They would rather hear, "This report is superb!" instead of "You did a nice job." They like to be in charge, and if they feel threatened, they will become defensive. Their worst fear is losing control — either of the situation or of themselves.

The L

Ls are motivated by acceptance. They want to be part of the group. They don't like dissension and would prefer not to rock the boat. If another employee takes credit for the L's work, the L will probably say nothing rather than address the issue.

Ls want everybody to be happy. If a group has decided to go to lunch, the High L will try to get everyone to agree on a restaurant. If things aren't going well, the L will give in and fall in line. They wear their hearts on their sleeves. They get their feelings hurt easily. Their worst fear is losing acceptance by other people. They are happy to follow the lead of others.

The F

High Fs are motivated by substance. Their decision style is methodical and sometimes slow. When trying to decide between two ties, the F compares the cost, the fabric and the craftsmanship. They need *all* the information before they can make a decision. When things don't go well, they tend to withdraw. Their worst fear is being wrong, which is why they don't take risks.

Now that you have taken the SELF Profile and studied the results, you can learn to flex your style and deal with others more effectively. If you have a communication problem with a co-worker or friend, review what you have learned to see if a change in the way you approach them might be helpful. Understanding both what motivates others and what turns them off allows you to move with confidence into situations where getting along with another person is vital.

INDEX

y any 3, get 1 FREE!

et a 60-Minute Training Series™ Handbook FREE ($14.95 value)*
you buy any three. See back of order form for full selection of titles.

hese are helpful how-to books for you, your employees and co-workers. Add to
library. Use for new-employee training, brown-bag seminars, promotion gifts and
, Choose from many popular titles on a variety of lifestyle, communication,
activity and leadership topics exclusively from National Press Publications.

DESKTOP HANDBOOK ORDER FORM

ing is easy:

omplete both sides of this Order Form, detach, and mail, fax or phone your order to:

Mail: National Press Publications
P.O. Box 419107
Kansas City, MO 64141-6107

ax: 1-913-432-0824
hone: 1-800-258-7248
nternet: www.NationalSeminarsTraining.com

lease print:

_____ Position/Title _____

any/Organization_____

ss_____City _____

Province_____ZIP/Postal Code _____

hone (____)_____ Fax (____) _____

e-mail: _____

asy payment:

nclosed is my check or money order for $_____ (total from back).
lease make payable to National Press Publications.

e charge to:
❏ MasterCard   ❏ VISA   ❏ American Express

t Card No. _____ Exp. Date_____

ture_____

● ●

MORE WAYS TO SAVE:

SAVE 33%!!! BUY 20-50 COPIES of any title ... pay just $9.95 each ($13.25 Canadian).

SAVE 40%!!! BUY 51 COPIES OR MORE of any title ... pay just $8.95 each ($11.95 Canadian).

* $20.00 in Canada

Buy 3, get 1 FREE!
60-MINUTE TRAINING SERIES™ HANDBOOKS

TITLE	ITEM #	RETAIL PRICE*	QTY	TOTAL
8 Steps for Highly Effective Negotiations	#424	$14.95		
Assertiveness	#4422	$14.95		
Balancing Career and Family	#4152	$14.95		
Common Ground	#4122	$14.95		
Delegate for Results	#4592	$14.95		
The Essentials of Business Writing	#4310	$14.95		
Everyday Parenting Solutions	#4862	$14.95		
Exceptional Customer Service	#4882	$14.95		
Fear & Anger: Slay the Dragons …	#4302	$14.95		
Fundamentals of Planning	#4301	$14.95		
Getting Things Done	#4112	$14.95		
How to Coach an Effective Team	#4308	$14.95		
How to De-Junk Your Life	#4306	$14.95		
How to Handle Conflict and Confrontation	#4952	$14.95		
How to Manage Your Boss	#493	$14.95		
How to Supervise People	#4102	$14.95		
How to Work With People	#4032	$14.95		
Inspire & Motivate: Performance Reviews	#4232	$14.95		
Listen Up: Hear What's Really Being Said	#4172	$14.95		
Motivation and Goal-Setting	#4962	$14.95		
A New Attitude	#4432	$14.95		
The New Dynamic Comm. Skills for Women	#4309	$14.95		
The Polished Professional	#4262	$14.95		
The Power of Innovative Thinking	#428	$14.95		
The Power of Self-Managed Teams	#4222	$14.95		
Powerful Communication Skills	#4132	$14.95		
Present With Confidence	#4612	$14.95		
The Secret to Developing Peak Performers	#4692	$14.95		
Self-Esteem: The Power to Be Your Best	#4642	$14.95		
Shortcuts to Organized Files & Records	#4307	$14.95		
The Stress Management Handbook	#4842	$14.95		
Supreme Teams: How to Make Teams Work	#4303	$14.95		
Thriving on Change	#4212	$14.95		
Women and Leadership	#4632	$14.95		

Sales Tax

All purchases subject to state and local sales tax. Questions? Call

1-800-258-7248

Subtotal	$
Add 7% Sales Tax *(Or add appropriate state and local tax)*	$
Shipping and Handling** *($6 one item; 50¢ each additional item)*	$
TOTAL	$

**Free Freight on all orders over $150.00   * $20.00 in Canada   0